Lead Or Be Lunch

DAVID VILLA

ISBN: 978-1-54391-169-5

DEDICATION

To my wife, Diana, my partner in marriage and business for over 24 years and the love of my life. For always encouraging me to keep going, and for never allowing me to cut corners. For exemplifying leadership in everything you do, and for never giving less than 100%. You are my single greatest inspiration and I cannot imagine how I could have made

it this far without you. Thank you

CONTENTS

PREFACE

For those who are not familiar with me, my name is David Villa. I am the CEO of a world class marketing agency known as iPD. In a period of 23 years, iPD has experienced times of immense success, as well as instances of extreme failure. As an entrepreneur and businessman, as a family-man, and as a follower of Christ, I felt that it was placed on my heart to share my tales of trials and tribulations as a leader. After two decades of working with the automotive industry, I feel that I would be doing others a disservice by not sharing the tips and tools of the trade that I have learned. If you have ever wondered what it was like to become a successful leader, or if you have ever thought about what being a strong leader would take, then this is the book for you. Leadership is not for the weak. It is not for the faint of heart, nor is it for those who lack tough skin. Leadership, or lack thereof, is something that will either make your business or break your business. My hope for those who are reading this is that this book will help you to make yours. My hope is that those who aspire to be a leader and those who want to strengthen their leadership skills will be able to take pointers from these pages, and apply them into their own lives.

I present to you Lead or Be Lunch: The Power of Earning Influence.

INTRODUCTION

The year is 1994. I am barely 22 years old, with a newborn daughter and a wife, and I am terrified. Terrified of how I am going to support my new family, terrified of what the future holds. Terrified of working tireless hours just to get by. Lately, I have been thinking and praying about something. Something crazy, something that I have always dreamed of, but not yet had the courage to attempt: I want to start my own business, and I wanted to focus my business on the aggressive, dog-eat-dog world that is the automotive industry.

You see, my father had become quite successful in this business. I felt like if I could just work hard at it, then I would be pretty much set after a couple of years or so! I was young and naïve, I had no idea that to accomplish such a task would take everything out of me. To me, the concept of a leader was just the person that hires people and tells them what to do. I did not yet understand the true meaning of a leader. Looking back today, I smile at the thought of it. A young guy who had almost no experience, but who had passion. The Dave that was in 1994 was hungry. He did not WANT to succeed, he HAD to succeed. He needed this to work. This was his last shot, his last hurrah.

To be honest, I had no other alternative. So I set out to chase this crazy dream, and today, almost 24 years later, I am still chasing, but from a much better starting position. After all of this time, I have learned how to do things and how not to do them. All of the success and failure, all of the people who have come and gone, every situation that I have been faced with was for a reason. I believe that God works in mysterious ways, and has taught me how to lead in an effective manner through these ups and downs that I have faced. This book is my way of jotting these instances down, and applying them to others who are involved or otherwise interested in becoming a strong, effective leader.

Leadership in any industry is not an easy job. It is stressful, and you are always on the clock. But every team needs a leader, and if not you then who? There is a finesse to being a leader, but there is no set path to follow. To be a solid leader, you will have to learn much of it on your own. But I believe that if you incorporate some of the aspects that we will discuss in later chapters, that you will have a much easier road ahead of you than if you simply go on your own and learn the hard way as I had. This book, and these stories and concepts in it, will be for you to learn from my mistakes, and for you to strengthen the parts of your approach to leadership that may need a bit of refining. These stories and ideas are purely from my heart and meant to help you in your quest to lead others. Whether you are looking to become a better leader of a small group, or looking to start your own business from the ground up, I believe that you will be able to find ideas in these pages that you will be able to utilize to your advantage in whatever it is that you decide to do in life.

In this book, I will help to teach you how to inspire rather than discourage, how to teach with actions rather than tell, how to help rather than hinder, and how to lead before you become lunch!

CHAPTER 1

Get Off the Bench

"You cannot fail, if you resolutely determine that you will not."
– Abraham Lincoln

I have often said, that where we ideally want to be, is in direct proportion to what we do and where we are at right now. This statement has proven truthful and as a matter of fact, this has been a catalyst in many areas of my personal–life as well as my career. So much of life, if not purposed, is spent watching it go by. A life that lacks purpose is similar to a football player who is sitting on the sidelines. They are looking at the game being played right before their eyes. The game is constantly changing. Players are going in and out, and various plays are going on. Despite our feelings and opinions, the game will continue with or without our participation. Are you itching to get off of the bench and participate? What part will you play? Or, a better question perhaps: What part do you envision yourself playing? What would be your ideal role?

I believe that, most of the time, it is a person's lack of involvement, which determines one's outcome of success. It isn't a lack of talent, or a lack of opportunity or handouts. It is the individual's own decision to not be fully involved. We all have big dreams. Many of us are talented. Opportunities and handouts (in some cases) can be abundant, but what you do with these gifts will ultimately define your experience. It will eventually determine whether or not you are victorious and successful. Imagine the football player, dressed in uniform from the helmet down to the socks and cleats. Your shoulder pads are on straight, and you anxiously bite down on your mouth guard. You have the look of a typical football player, but are you actually ready to get out onto the field and play the game? By the time you have determined whether your heart is in it and you are ready, it is already the fourth quarter and the game is winding down to an end, yet you do not have a single grass stain on you. Why?

You may have some talent, or opportunity has afforded you the ability to be a player. Like some, you may even have had more than enough schooling or continuous training. Yet here you are, standing on the sidelines. You are clean and untouched by the game playing out right before your very eyes. Apprehension and fear are paralyzing emotions and can silently defeat you without your notice. That is because they are preventative emotions. They prevent you from trying and ultimately winning. Remember that getting off of the bench has less to do with talent, or what has been afforded to us, but rather what we are actually doing with those gifts. Are you afraid to jump because you might fall? It is certain that the chance of failure exists, but so does the chance of success. You will not know what you are actually capable of until you try. I am here right now to encourage all who is reading this to GET OFF OF THE BENCH!

I am a father of three. I can vividly remember when my kids were little and just learning how to swim. For the parents reading this, you will know exactly what I am talking about. I would be in the pool while they stood at the edge, frozen with fears. Their eyes would be big and wide, and they would only stare back in silence, watching me in the water. They wanted so badly to be in the water, but were unsure of what exactly would occur if they decided to let go of their inhibitions. I would swim up to them with my arms outstretched, encouraging them to jump, explaining that I would be right there to catch them as soon as they hit the water. This tactic, however, did little to make things easier for them. It was not because they did not trust me, but rather this act of jumping into the water would require more than faith. It would require them to take action. As a kid, this would be one aspect of their life only they had control over. Action, as we all know, is always scarier when doing something for the first time. Luckily, my kids decided to let go and jump. They have not stopped swimming since! The look on each of their faces upon realizing that they were safe and unharmed is a priceless memory of mine.

I happen to believe that there is no secret recipe to achieving success. There is, however, a key component that is required to achieve your goals. That key component is action. Success can be measured by an accumulation of actions set forth by you every single day. That will put you one step closer to achieving your overall goal. People neglect taking action because it requires actual work to be done. There is nothing glamorous about it at times, and it is not always the most fun thing to do. It will always be the correct thing if you want to find any level of success in your endeavors.

It is absolutely necessary to take persistent, massive action upon pursuit of greatness. Likewise, it's important to maximize your success and achieve specific goals. Action will require you to get out of your comfort zone and into the game, even when you may not feel like it. There are absolutely ZERO shortcuts to success. As human beings, it is not out of the ordinary to look for a way to cut corners so you will not have to use so much effort. In order to live out your dreams, you must make moves. It is easy to neglect the tasks that require the most effort, but do not be that type of player. Be any player but the one who is left sitting on the sidelines. Do not take your dreams and sit on the bench and pout. If getting off of the bench still scares you, look inside yourself for something to believe in. Use that as a crutch to propel you forward. We all have untapped abilities and qualities. Recognizing these strengths will allow you to better focus on something that you may need to work on.

I am a firm believer that talent alone won't cut it. Potential does not matter. You can develop your talent and you can unlock your potential; but, you cannot train or teach persistence. In fact, I will take persistence over talent any day of the week. If two individuals walked into my office for interviews for the same job function, and one was highly talented and the other was extremely determined–I would choose the determined candidate ten times out of time. The determined and persistent candidate's inability to give up, or take "no" for an answer, will go a much further distance than the talented one. Your talent, like the talents of others, can be developed and perfected. Unabashed persistence cannot be trained, nonetheless; yet, you will almost certainly succeed. Persistence reflects progress, no matter the outcome.

One of my favorite quotes on this subject comes from one of the NBA's all time greats, Michael Jordan. He explained it like this: "I've missed more than nine thousand shots in my career. I have lost almost three hundred games. Twenty–six times, I've been trusted to take the game winning shot, and missed. I've failed over and over and over again in my life. And that is why I succeed."

Those who are afraid to fail will coast through their life, never coming close to reaching their full potential. Failure, despite genuine effort, is an underrated teacher and motivator. It is a sign that one is striving at close to full capacity.

There will be times where taking massive action is the last thing that you will feel like doing. Find ways to fire yourself up. You, like my kids who were standing on the side of the pool, might be afraid to jump in. You cannot allow fear to para-lyze you. Some time ago, I came across an acronym for the word "fear" and it has stuck with me. The acronym has al-lowed me to better be able to conquer the things that cause me to be the most afraid. It is simply this: **F**alse **E**vidence **A**ppear-ing **R**eal.

Let's break this down. Fear is, quite simply, the presentation of false information appearing real to you in order to make you feel afraid. If this acronym is true, then the subject of your fear is simply appearing to you as something much scarier than it actually is. Knowing this should make it exceptionally easier to conquer. It is less likely to subdue you in your pursuits to lead! Allowing yourself to let go of your preliminary fears will re-ward you ten–fold, simply by making the start easier for you every time action is required in the future.

Hang your most important goal somewhere where you will be able to see it on a daily basis. Talk yourself through it. What-ever you have to do–make sure you are constantly searching for ways to fire yourself up for it. Keep yourself in the game. Let the competition fall off and become complacent, but do not allow yourself to do the same under any circumstances. Mas-sive success does not come overnight. If you are willing to wake up each morning, and declare that you are going to com-pete with the person you were yesterday, then you will be well on your way.

When I was younger in my career, I was still working for my father. The one thing that I was the most afraid of was letting go of my lifeline, for I was starting to work on my dream of owning my own business. At the time, I was in a position where I was stable and starting to make great money. I was presented with the decision to stay right where I was, or I could attempt to venture out onto something that was unknown. In the unknown was where I would find my dream. Everything at this point in my life was laid out before me. I was in a secure place, both personally as well as professionally, yet here I was—drowning in uncertainty and fear over what I should do. I could choose the option that perfectly laid out my future, or I could venture off down the road less traveled and work towards my own goals, with an unknown and uncertain outcome. I decided to choose the path of uncertainty. The entire world opened up to me. Everything form this point on was an adventure. By this, I do not mean that everything was perfect by anyone's standards. I had to fail over and over again, in order to find myself, and to find my dream realized. I had gone from experiencing consistent success and financial security, to road blocks, unexpected challenges, and more failures. In fact, if I recounted to you in detail each of the times that I experienced failure, the list would end up longer than this entire book.

Your goals shouldn't scare you. If they do not scare you, then the outcome is probably not going to be extraordinary. The fear of the outcome is necessary, and indicative of the challenge that has been laid out before you. Overcoming that fear is not only required. It is actually much easier to face than you imagined. Get off of the bench and face what scares you the most. Your persistence in your endeavors is the only thing that you need to hold on to in order to get yourself back up during the times when failure tries to take you down.

One of our nations greatest leaders, Abraham Lincoln, is a true testimony to the metaphor of "getting in the game." He absolutely fulfilled the idea that anyone can make it in America. Abraham Lincoln was a man of little means and a poor education. He was born in a one–room log cabin. It was this humble upbringing that made Lincoln an honest and hard–working man. Lincoln overcame numerous obstacles and failures in order to become the President of the United States, during a time in which the nation would be confronted with one of its gravest catastrophes.

Yet Abraham Lincoln was not always viewed as a winner. He failed so often that it is a wonder how he cemented his place in history at all! Many of you may not know that Abraham Lincoln began his political career in 1832, but he would not be elected president until 1860. In the 28 years which spanned his political career, Abraham Lincoln:

- lost his job

- was defeated in state legislature

- failed in his business career

- his lifelong sweetheart died

- had a nervous breakdown

- was defeated for House Speaker

- defeated for nomination for Congress

- lost re–nomination

- was rejected for land officer

- defeated for nomination for Vice President of the United States

- was defeated for Senate

- and then, he was elected PRESIDENT!

All of this occurred following the death of his mother at a very early age, which resulted in a very poor upbringing.

Throughout his life, Lincoln was faced with defeat. The truest testament to his character, and ultimately what granted him his place in U.S. History, is the fact that he never gave up. His road to the White House is one of the greatest examples of persistence that I personally have ever read. Over time Lincoln would lose eight elections and fail twice in business. He suffered a nervous breakdown, but this did not deter him from his political career. There isn't much that should derail you from achieving your dreams of success. Lincoln became a champion because he was unafraid. Let go of your fear and get in the game. Become your own story of persistence!

I will say it again: Where a person currently stands is relative to where they desire to be in life. To me, this statement defines not only a dream, but cements one's future as a visionary. If you can envision yourself and your future, then the investment you are making for your passion will solidify your dedication for your craft. Ask yourself if your dream is what you really want to see come to fruition. If the answer is yes, then everything you do today should enable you to get to where you want to be tomorrow. I encourage you to stop waiting for advantageous moments. Instead, be the pioneer and create movement on your own.

Visionaries keep envisioning their dreams. This happens in an expanding, forward movement. They are constantly adding to their objectives, sometimes before they even complete what they initially set out to do. Visionaries live today, yesterday! Vision always proceeds action. What was yesterday's vision is being lived out right now. Because something is only a vision at the time, and has yet come to reality, it can be an addition or adjustment to a more refined goal. A visionaries' ambitions and dreams are always being edited or revised. You must take the actions necessary to live your dream and continue to add to it. Look back to what you have in your hands. Use what is in them to propel you forward. Use your vision to keep you constantly changing. Do not stay the same. Allow your dream to get bigger. More importantly, permit your dream to keep repeating itself in larger forms. Always keep the seeds to your greatness in your hand. You can continue to plant them for a better tomorrow.

In order to help rid yourself of apprehension and fear, there are a few things that I recommend doing before leaping to action. The first is to create a plan for their vision. According to conventional wisdom, the first thing every visionary must do is to first create a plan for the vision itself. This plan usually describes the size of the dream, the problems that will need to be resolved along the way, and a solution that the dream will provide. Having a vision plan is essentially a research exercise written in isolation at a desk, before the visionary has even begun to build a product. It is possible to figure out most of the unknowns of a dream in advance, before you execute the vision.

Next, find what I call a "dream incubator." This should be a confidant who listens and dreams with you. We all need a shoulder to lean on, and sometimes a shoulder to cry on. Someone there to support us through all of the challenging times and builds us up when we need it the most. It is very possible that, without the help of my dream incubators, I may have not achieved the level of success for which I have experienced.

Once you have your vision plan and your dream incubator, you should then get to work on executing your plan with diligence and persistence. When you find failure, don't let it keep you down for long! When unexpected road blocks present themselves in front of you, take a moment to rest, reset, and revisit your blueprints. Refocus your energy on your "why." Why are you here? Why is this dream important to you? Why must you continue?

As the CEO of iPD, our internal theme at the company is "ALL IN." There are visions and goals, both personal and corporate, which are in front of us. In order to reach those summits, we must not go about things haphazardly. Rather, we should be invested fully by giving one hundred percent in everything that we do. It is my belief that all of us possess God given talents and abilities that only we can use. I want to remind you again to look at what is placed before you and inside you. God has given gifts to each of us that vary greatly.

Many of us face obstacles on a daily basis that seem insurmountable. However, we have been equipped with the ability to accomplish success and reach the finish line. Whatever is already in you, I assure you, that it is all you need to get started on your dreams and your vision.

Look at a flourishing fruit tree that is fully grown and full of luscious fruit. It may stand twenty feet tall, with thousands of leaves and ripe fruit, but it was not always so large and impressive. This tree first began as a seed. Sometime long ago, perhaps a farmer planted it. The farmer had to stand over freshly toiled soil, and took the seed from his burlap sack. The farmer placed the seeds in the ground, and over time, the earth nurtured those seeds until the tree flourished. Only then, would the farmer be able to eat the fruit that the little seed produced, taking the literal fruits from his labor. We hold the seeds that can eventually grow into our dreams, our visions, our goals, and our aspirations.

So what is the key? Be ALL IN! You have to be active in your pursuits and your endeavors. You have to consistently propel yourself and your goals in perpetual forward motion. You have to consistently take massive, vigorous action to conquer what it is that you are chasing. The key is to take what we posses and to actively give it all we've got. We cannot hold back, as it will take everything that we have. What do you have? How can you use it in pursuit of your own destiny? I love a quote that Napoleon said, "what the mind can conceive and believe in, the mind can achieve." If you believe in yourself and believe in your dreams, then you can achieve absolutely everything that you set out for. Ask yourself, am I all in? If you are not giving one hundred percent, then the answer to that question is no.

When you are all in and fully involved, your end results will be incredible.

In no–limit poker, to bet all of your chips is a sign of total confidence in what is in your hand. If you have a very good hand, you go all–in so that you can win the maximum amount, or to simply scare off mediocre hands so they won't catch the cards that they need to win. The only person who knows your dream is you. The only one who can see it realized is you. You are the common denominator.

The Bible says:

"God has given each of us the ability to do certain things well."

Paul emphasized that we're to actually use these gifts and abilities, as God has given us them for the benefit of those around us. Some people may say, "I don't know what to do" or "I don't really have any special talent to give." Moses said the exact same thing when God spoke to him at the burning bush. But God explained to Moses that he had more than enough to accomplish what it was that God had set him out to accomplish. Like Moses, you have to take what you have and use it. You have to be all in!

Theodore Roosevelt once said:

"Do what you can, with what you have, where you are."

He was not wrong. Everything that you need to flourish is in you already. Trust the blessings that you are holding, and use them. You have dreams, aspirations, and a vision for the future. You would not be reading this book if you didn't, right? Well, are you ready to get off of the bench? My best advice to you would be to take inventory of your dreams and visions, get off of the bench, and get back into the game! Nothing has the power to stop you but you.

"For I know the plans I have for you" declares the Lord. "Plans to prosper you and not to harm you, plans to give you hope and a future." – Jeremiah 29:11

CHAPTER 2

Culture of Purpose

"An extraordinary business starts with extraordinary people. Extraordinary people start with purpose." – Jesper Lowgren

I have been a CEO for nearly twenty years. I often get asked of the most important concepts which I have learned while working in business. The answer is simple: company culture. Your culture is everything to your business. Identifying and building upon that culture starts with its leader. Leadership is about what you do and what you say. A healthy company culture is evidence of a leader who understands how important it truly is to inspire those on his or her team. They lead and live as an example. A great leader will not only be vocal about their goals, but everything that they say is then backed by action. What you say and what you do must align. When you have set this as the standard, the team and those around you will follow.

Every leader has the ideal vision of running an organization where everything goes smoothly. Everyone is happy, likes their coworkers, and has fun without much effort. But as we all know, the reality of the situation is very different. A leader has to work together to push everyone in the right direction. Leaders must make sure they lead by example, while they define their company's culture. In most cases, culture is shaped by how leadership acts. You will have to make sure that your leadership team embodies the type of organization that you want to be. For instance, if "team culture" is your aim, your executive team truly needs to know how to work as a team.

In this chapter, I will discuss how great leaders and businesses serve their calling to solve problems. They understand they have a purpose which can actually make a meaningful difference in the lives of those they lead. Being the living, breathing example of your dream is an inspiring way to rally those around you to walk in purpose. It is not enough to just have a goal or target to meet. It is not enough to simply wish for something. Wish lists will not get you to where you're trying to go. Once again, it all comes down to taking massive action.

Let your words be your plan. Let your words be the blueprint to your success. Get moving and calculate each of the movements that help to propel you forward as you go. Send the invite to your team and bring them with you. People with passion have no problem being active. It is these people that are going to be the drivers in your organization. Use your and their abilities to drive your organization to the next destination. Once you have reached the goal, take a moment to regroup and assess the next steps…and then keep moving.

Great performance can never come without great people and culture. The opposite is also true. Great people and culture will only be affiliated with the highest performing organizations. We can argue over which drives the other, but regardless, there is one undeniable truth: when a company is in its earliest days —when there are performances or numbers of which to speak —the key differences are: the team, their purpose, and their culture.

Many leaders often realize the importance of a healthy company culture only when it is already too late. It is crucial to identify and install the values and ideals of your organization as early in the game as possible. When your business starts to grow, these ingrained standards stay with the company. When it comes to company culture, it is important to take a close look at your organization's chemical makeup. I like to refer to this as your company's DNA. Your company DNA is an identifier of the heart and soul of your business, your team, and your vision. Like your own genetic makeup, your company DNA cannot be modified or manufactured. The foundation is natural and flows organically. I highly recommend taking the time to identify this important part of your company culture. It should be used as the sounding board to compare the progress of your success.

Your company DNA can also refer to how you **Develop Natural Alignment**. In other words, how you build a strong, positive corporate culture in the modern business world. When a company has a great culture, they are hands–down more productive. When a business is more productive, it means that it is working faster. As a result, it will get a leg up on the competition. When I began to focus on the importance of culture, I realized that employees started to care about an organization's purpose rather than simply collecting a paycheck. I learned that employees who are convinced of a larger common goal, are also the people who are excited to be part of the larger purpose.

When your corporate DNA is healthy, every component of your business moves forward in harmony. Rather than existing in separate, uncommunicative silos–your team members work together towards a common purpose. Through trial and error, I have found these four major points helpful in creating company culture that lasts, all while creating a culture that wins.

1. **Unleash Innovation**

   Every stellar idea is born of innovation, but how do you foster an innovative environment? First, ask your team members. Challenge the individuals who work in your business day in and day out to uncover new and better ways to do things. What are better methods for pleasing customers? Your employees are front and center to the action and are most likely to spot opportunities for innovation. Often, they simply need a bit of encouragement in order to get those ideas out in the open.

I am here to tell you that unleashing innovation will be challenging. It is most definitely possible to do. I admit that there are areas in which I find myself struggling; this has always been one of them. I make mistakes and continue to fail, but I still persist until I do find success. I encourage you to do the same. Working collaboratively with your employees, and those who are around you will allow you to foster an innovative environment for ideas. As a leader, it is important to be open to criticism, ideas, and opinions. Give your people a safe place to share their own unique thoughts. This is a concept that we will go into further detail later on.

The number one reason a leader tends to fail at unleashing their innovation is due to a lack of ambition. They do not recognize how to embrace their talent, nor are they loyal to their team. Creating a company culture where your employees feel valued, and given enough space to allow their own unique ideas is key. Your team needs to trust that they are being heard, and that their leader is just as loyal to them as they are to their leader. Refusal to embrace your team will ultimately result in failure. You will find yourself back at the drawing board, one step further away from realizing your dreams.

Setting up regular brainstorming meetings, in which you generate multiple product ideas, is also a great way to promote innovation amongst the employees. Involve a diverse group of people from different teams and different areas of your company. Stress that all ideas are welcome. It's as simple as this: you want to get people's attention and get them to start thinking. Once they trust that their ideas can be shared in a safe place, the innovation will soon began to flow.

Additionally, streamline your team meetings. Clearly state the reason for the meeting in advance. Make sure that all participants know the agenda and how they should prepare themselves. Everyone in your company needs to be on the same page.

2. **Develop a Clear Mission and Vision**

At the heart of every great company is a clear sense of purpose. Young people just now entering into the workforce want to understand your company's values. They're looking for a culture of purpose. To develop core beliefs, values, and customs. Your company leaders must commit to a shared vision that has an impact beyond your own company. Where culture and purpose meet, you'll find the most vibrant, successful companies of the modern era.

Developing a vision and mission statement is crucial to the success of community and company initiatives. These statements should explain your aspirations in a concise manner. Help your company and its employees focus on what is really important. Provide a basis for developing other aspects of your strategic plan.

It is important that your company develops a vision and mission statement for a number of reasons. These statements can help your company focus on what is really important. Although you may know what you are trying to accomplish, it is sometimes easy to lose sight of this when dealing with the day–to–day hustle. Your vision and your mission statement will help your employees and those in your community remember what is most important, as you go about your daily grind.

Also, your vision and mission statements let others see a snapshot view of your company. It clarifies what you are striving to accomplish. When your vision and mission is clearly and easily visible, it allows people to learn about who you are without having to work hard for the information.

Lastly, your vision and mission statements will help focus and bind your teammates together. Not only are these statements important to company culture, but the process of developing them will allow your team to feel united. The most important take away from this: people will believe in something more completely if they believe they had a hand in developing it themselves.

Your corporate culture starts with you–the leader. A leader has to build its house on top of its core foundation. This consists of beliefs, ambitions, and goals. Creating a mission statement is an opportunity to lay out your vision and goals for making sound decisions. The best mission statements define a company's goals in at least three dimensions:

- how the company serves its customers

- how the company meets its employees' needs

- what the company does for its owners

A culture of purpose is essentially the atmosphere that is created through a group of people. Each person is centered on collaborating together on the same goal. Being that purpose is the common denominator. This group of people should understand their differences, but each use them to their individual advantage. In turn, this promotes one another toward the same place or the same dream.

3. **Win the Battle for Talent**

How can you attract more than your fair share of the top talent in your field? Well, it is going to take a lot more than just money. That is not to say that money is not important; of course people care about it and are often driven by it. But if motivation was only about making money, the best people would bail out as soon as they realized that they could make more elsewhere. Something else drives them to carry on, even in the face of adversity. Many of the most talented workers will switch their focus form the external to their own personal growth and happiness and live off of what fuels their passion.

The best people–those who you want to seek and retain–are motivated by passion. I have found that most people do their best work when they are passionately engaged in what they are doing. Passionate people are the best because they use their passion as fuel to take their vision places. Those without passion tend to be complacent and camp out in their comfort zone. If passion is the fuel to drive one ahead in life, then those without it may simply not be moving forward. Those that hang out in "Comfortville" are not necessarily in a bad place, but it is never THE place if someone wants to actually reap the fruits of their labor. Instead, those that use their passions as a catalyst to fuel their movement will almost always find themselves instead in "Fruitville." Fruitville references the place where passionate and driven people go to see their dreams become realities. It is also the place that you want to go to find and win the battle for talent.

So how do you spot these individuals? Passion is a confident smile and a proactive attitude. These types usually think outside of themselves and for the greater good. They often work outside of what is defined in their job description, frequently step outside of their comfort zone. They take the time to help those around them. These talented, passionate types are your wildcards, your culture ambassadors. They are the keys to your company culture, and play a validating role in the organization's success.

People do their best work when they're passionately engaged. Passion provides us with purpose in our work, but it also give us purpose in our lives. It makes us feel like we're on the right path in our lives, and it gives us hope for a happy and exciting future.

4. Embrace Your Frontline "Culture Ambassadors"

Before the title "culture ambassador" became a staple in the business world lexicon, these employees were generally known as your organization's "wildcards." There has always been an unknown need and desire for these styles of employees. Nobody really knew what to call them at the time. Culture Ambassadors are the employees making waves, growing fast, and standing out form the crowd. These types of employees help their leaders (and their team members) rethink strategies, while also helping reinvent the approach to innovation.

Your company's "culture ambassadors" are those who care the most about your mission and values. They are willing to communicate with a strong passion. They are absolutely crucial for fostering strong work cultures which retain key employees and attract top talent. They can show you how to move forward by rethinking strategies, reinventing approaches to innovation, reconnecting with customers and rediscovering the power that employees have to lead the charge towards positive changes.

Keep People at the Center

Chances are, you're a leader within an industry which strives to put its people first. Therefore, it should go without saying that good people skills are simply nonnegotiable for your company. Identify and build healthy corporate DNA by getting clear on your mission and vision. Encourage innovation at all costs, while attracting and retaining talented team members. Create an environment in which your culture ambassadors can thrive.

Keep your people at the center of your company culture by embracing their ideas. Acknowledge their successes, and fostering an environment in which continued education, alongside growth is possible. If there is not a platform in which your team feels safe to share their ideas, your turnover rate may be high and you may find that everyone coming to work is simply showing up to clock in and clock out and collect a paycheck.

These types of employees will come in and leave right on time. They typically do not smile at their desks, nor do they talk about their work very much. They may only come to work because they have to get paid. Instead, find a team that comes to work every day because they enjoy it. Give your employees the outlet to find their "it" and help them along the way while they do so. Helping others around you to find their purpose in their work, and in your company culture, will almost always result in success. This is not only true for you and your organization, but for them and their personal lives as well.

Celebrate your team. Embrace their passion for your company; help them define their purpose. What gets celebrated can help to define the culture. The more that you recognize the specific behaviors that reinforce your culture and how your employees engage in it, the better. Tie recognition to the team and company strategy so that values and culture can be reinforced with every celebration. Whether it be a sale, or an idea, take the time to acknowledge those that are walking in purpose with you toward the same goal.

You will need three different types of "power people" on your team. I believe that the crucial, immediately effective recipe that can make the difference between a team that fails and a team that succeeds involves the people itself. If you are leading a team of more than a few people, chances are that you probably already have the ingredients for an amazing team already within your reach.

As a good leader, you already known that each and every member of your team is individually important. And you have probably chosen those people with great care and consideration for the future of your company. But if you have not yet already considered it, now is the time to look even more closely at the team that you have built up so far. A leader cannot go at it alone. If you have been trying to fulfill that role on your own, you have probably begun to see how difficult that will become.

One of these three different types of power people would be the visionary. As a leader of your team, you probably fit into this role yourself. This does not necessarily have to be the case, as you could potentially fill any of the three roles. But, if you can recognize that you are not the visionary of this team, it is up to you to find the person who is or who can be. Visionaries are never satisfied with "now." This absolutely does not mean that visionaries are not happy or grateful. Rather, by never being satisfied, visionaries never seem to stop. They are constantly working at making things better, and looking on the brighter side of things. The visionaries of your company will be the driving force for the future of the entire team.

The next of the three different types of power people would be the tender–hearted. This key player on your leadership team nurtures everyone around them. He or she is the one who is constantly lifting up and helping the team make it. When the visionary comes across a little too hot, your tender–hearted team member is the one who cools them down and conveys the heart within their information to the rest of the team, pulling everyone together. It is easy to see why someone who can naturally fill this quietly powerful position is crucial to the success of the entire team.

The final type of power people that you will find amongst your team is the doer. This is your team member who is fanatical about executing the ideas of the visionary. The team visionary talks and pushes forward big ideas, the tender–hearted nurturer helps everyone else understand and deal with the ideas, and the doer is the one who picks up the ideas and runs with it. A doer lays down the hard labor and effort to accomplish the tasks that are laid out before them. He or she understands and executes the big ideas so that they become action. Without the doer, things just never seem to get done as well or as quickly. The doer on your team is key to ensuring that the big ideas are never in doubt.

With these three important roles covered, you will immediately start to see positive results in your team. Remember that the first person you hire represents the foundation for the twentieth person you hire. Foster an environment that supports collaboration and discussion between everyone on the team. Be a successful leader of change and cast your vision for your team. Ensure that the vision and goals are clear by answering any questions that your team has for you. You cannot succeed by sending your team through an issue. You have to identify, embrace, and guide them through it. This can only be achieved through very clear and open communication.

A great leader is also someone that is willing and able to lay their ego down. Ego does play a big role in your success, but it is not in your accomplishments. Instead, it is in your ability to put your ego in the back seat when necessary. Ego does not need to be the star. Rather, make it a faceless actor. Only embrace it when it is absolutely necessary. Great leaders do not build a team of yes men (or yes women), and they do not hold onto the mindset that as a leader. They have the "Midas touch." Not everything you touch will turn to god and not every attempt at success will be victorious. Failure and struggle will be abundant throughout the journey toward your dream. However, if you surround yourself with the right people who identify and believe in your company culture as much as you do, then the journey won't be nearly as lonely or uncomfortable as it could be.

Leaders produce leaders. Your team will always follow your lead until they outgrow you, but it is important to know that you can continue to lead while allowing your team to grow and lead as well. The goal is not to create followers but instead, to reproduce leaders. The fruit of leadership grows on the trees of those around you. This is the only way to grow personally and professionally. Create a culture of purpose and find those culture ambassadors to walk in significance with you. I guarantee, that with the right people by your side, you can do no wrong.

"Arise, for it is your task, and we are with you; be strong and do it" – Ezra 10:4

CHAPTER 3

Assembling A Mosaic

"Good teams become great ones when the members trust each other enough to surrender the me for the we." – Phil Jackson

When I began to think of the idea and theme of this chapter, I started to think about the idea of working as a team. It reminded me of an old fable that my father had once told me about the chicken and the pig. It is a story of the idea of commitment to a cause, and how important it is to recognize the difference between someone being involved and someone's full sacrifice. This is a story that stuck with me. I knew that I wanted to share it with you when the time came to write about assembling your team.

There are many different adaptations of the fable, but I will tell it in the way my father told it to me. To make a long story short, the chicken suggests that he and the pig involve themselves in a scheme that involves making bacon and eggs. The pig, after some thought, replies and notes that for the chicken, only a small contribution of a couple of eggs is required. Yet for the pig, in order to make bacon, he must give up his life and be slaughtered in order to complete his part of the bargain. For the pig, this is a complete sacrifice, while for the chicken, laying some eggs is only a small contribution and minor inconvenience for him.

This fable can be used as a metaphor to show the difference between two different types of people in which you may come across as a leader. There are those who, like the pigs, are key people totally committed and accountable for outcomes of success. Then, there are those who are like the chickens. They consult, inform, and are involved in the production of ideas within the company. Understand that a successful team will need both types of individuals in order to prosper. While it was the pigs full sacrifice in the story, it was the chicken's idea that started the plan originally. Ideas, innovation, and involvement are all necessary when it comes to projects. Listen to the ideas and incorporate them into ta project where you feel they may fit best. This will not only keep workers feeling fulfilled and happy, but it will keep you moving forward. It is wide to make sure that your company culture welcomes and is open to collaborating with these types of individuals. Given the sacrifice required of being the type who are willing to take the form of the pig in the story, this type of person will provide to be difficult to find and even more difficult to retain. In turn, the construction of a successful team must ensure that the project has sufficient individuals who fit this category, and ensure that they are empowered to drive the project in return for committing to and taking accountability for it.

In order to gain this type of commitment from your team, it is imperative that you first assemble the right people and put each of the right pieces in its place. This starts with having leadership define, identify, attract and retain the right people. Look for the types of employees that fill the appropriate role within your company. This will include the "chickens" and "pigs" of your organization. Each role filled should be customized based on the role each team member plays.

So, with that said and kept in mind, let's take a moment to look over and discuss hiring, building, and managing a team in today's business world. I like to compare this process to that of assembling a mosaic. A mosaic is a surface decoration made by inlaying small pieces of diverse elements to form pictures or patterns. Every individual that you encounter will be unique and have their own set of skills which differentiates them from one another. If we are, in a sense, assembling a mosaic, then the finished product needs to be a great team that is putting forth the effort. "The effort" may be making cold calls, getting through the lunch rush, constructing a building before the deadline, or delivering well on the presentation and closing the deal. If you have worked hard in whatever industry that you are in, and managed to assemble all of your key people–then great! You have all of the pieces of greatness that you will need. However, success doesn't stop there. You should always be in a state of growth and reassessment. You should be continuously asking yourself the following questions: Do all of these pieces fit? Am I possibly missing out on any additional pieces? How can I continue to add these key pieces to my team?

I encourage you to try and be open–minded when making this decision. Do not overlook the many diverse talents and qualities that are available to you in the market today. I personally have learned (through many mistakes unfortunately) that there are talented and successful professionals out there that are not necessarily like me. These professionals, if given the opportunity, a reputable product to sell, and an earning potential that is motivating, can accomplish far more than I could have ever expected, in multiple separate areas.

It is through diversity. Team diversity specifically, that this mosaic will start to come together. A point of difference, a variety of talents, along with a leader who understands that to accomplish what is dreamed is only possible through a team. It is said that, "there is no I in team," but understand that you can find a ME in the word team, if you move things around a bit. This concept of no I in team has never sat well with me. A team in itself is a grouping of INDIVIDUALS, each with their own separate set of gifts and skills. Each person is a complement those around them, when properly used together. As leaders who are trying to put the pieces together, we must look for the pieces that will become more than just a simple collection of people. The right people will bring a strong sense of mutual commitment, creating the synergy needed to generate something greater than the sum of the performance of each individual member! If you can apply this to the team, the finished product will have shifted the typical team balance from that of disruption and uproar, to that of a symphonic orchestra, where each voice is heard in unison, complementing one another. Each instrument plays their own part under the director's leadership, and they, in turn, create a masterpiece.

Now that you have the correct people on your team, and you understand each of their specialized traits and skill sets, it is time that we talk about how to collaborate with them. Your team is important and so are their ideas. If you truly want to achieve greatness, then your key people should be there for you to utilize to help propel everyone there. This is what leveraging creative collaboration is all about.

I know that we all can have a tendency to look at this profession as "one size fits all," yet, I have found over time that this could not be much further from the actual truth. A "one size fits all" profession is one where creativity, innovation, and growth simply do not exist. These professions generally operate under what is called a "top–down" philosophy. It stems from the person at the top's "my way or the highway" mentality. Commonly called pyramid schemes by many, they do not often promote growth or any real idea of promotion within them.

Today, the biggest breakthroughs seem to happen when people with a collective vision join together and share ideas, information, and work. Most top CEOs don't do all of the work themselves. Their success as an individual has now put them in a position where they are able to hire others who can work together to accomplish a single goal.

Consider Kodak's George Fisher as an example, brought in after a highly publicized firing of the former CEO, Kay Whitmore. George Fisher was greeted with significant optimism during a period of very poor performance for the company. He was brought in with hopes that he would be able to turn the company around for the better, but even his level of charisma could not single–handedly revolutionize the company at the time.

As the CEO of an expanding marketing agency, I have done it both ways. Ten years ago, when I was about halfway into my career, I was working under the philosophy of "the boss knows best" and over a period of just one month, eight managers had left, mainly because of the fact that their ideas were not shared and were ignored. I had stifled their voice, and my business had suffered as a result. It took me actually losing quality people who were key figured to realize that I was learning my lesson the hard way. The lone ranger approach that I had once stuck by had failed me. It ended up being a blessing in disguise to learn this sooner rather than later. In order for me to see the vision I had inside me come to fruition, I would have to be willing to collaborate with the incredible talent that I had surrounded myself with all along.

Collaboration is the key element for businesses who are embarking on the "good to great" journey. This will entail more than just people working together. The entire process as a whole is what YOU make it. In other words, you must bring certain attributes as a leader to the table in order to set the foundation for success. This includes learning how to coach appropriately. Bringing down the hammer is necessary at times, but keep in mind what bringing down the hammer has the potential to do; break a solid foundation. Take the same route as many successful sports coaches: you have to inspire and motivate in order to form a strong team or foundation.

A great deal of my success, for example, can be attributed to the principles that I, myself, adopted years ago. One such mentor of mine was John Maxwell, CEO of iNJOY. He once said: "Leadership is not about titles, positions, or flowcharts. It is simply about one life influencing another." His statement struck a chord in me. I have tried to apply the same type of philosophy to both my work and my personal life ever since. Being an influential leader, motivating your team, and capitalizing on each person's varying strengths will help you achieve your goal. Though it doesn't stop there. You will also need to know how to recognize potential when listening to another person's ideas. As team members identify and explore their own strengths, weaknesses, and skills–they will gain an understanding of how they can combine the various skills amongst the group. They will also begin to understand how utilizing the varying skills will contribute to greater success of everyone.

A strong and effective leader is able to unite and motivate the team, while also possessing the ability to make an authoritative decision. When working collaboratively, a final decision will need to be made at some point. As a leader, your ability to follow through with that decision will be what sets you apart from the rest. People are not going to work with you or believe you, if they cannot trust you. Never give false hope and don't worry about sugar coating the truth. If you want to develop solid relationships amongst your team, and prove that you are trustworthy, then this is crucial. When communicating, remain optimistic and speak effectively. Speak in a clear and concise manner. Doing so will allow you to engage and connect with employees on a personal level, which will, in turn, further fostering an environment of respect and trust.

Creative collaboration is simple when you have leverage. When you utilize the ideas and assistance of others, it takes less time. Even the most significant dreams will become obtainable through the usage of creative collaboration.

Think of your goals as boxes, standing in your way. Some are light and easily moved, yet some are heavy and will require a lot of effort on your part in order to remove them from your path. You know that you can move them and get to where you need to go, but will it be worth it? Will you achieve the amount of success that you initially dreamt of without the heavy lifting?

When you set large goals, and have huge dreams of success, the objects in your way will likely be much heavier and a lot larger. The large boxes will surely be in the way of what is a large dream and vision. You're either going to need multiple people or a lever in order to lift the objects in front of you. Either way, moving these boxes requires something or someone other than yourself. These big dreams are worth it, but anyone who has achieved success will tell you that it is going to require a team of people to move the weight and help you get through.

The definition of cohesion is "the action or fact of forming a united whole." A team is said to be in a state of cohesiveness when its members stick together and remain united in the pursuit of a common goal. It is your job, as a leader, to bring cohesion to your team. You have to serve them as their motivator and peace maker. To do this, let's take a look at a few important things to encourage cohesion amongst team members and what to when conflict arises.

The first key for cohesion would be open communication. We have already discussed this loosely, but we, as leaders, should know that communication is key in successful team and relationship building. Leaders and team managers should encourage their workers to communicate regularly with one another. One way to help develop methods to aid in a team's communication is to allow them to meet with one another regularly. Rather than setting meeting times, allow your people to keep open lines of communication, both with you and each other. As a leader, you do not need to meet with everyone all the time. By keeping an "open door policy" whenever you can, it will allow your team the opportunity to speak with you as well as other members of your leadership team whenever they need assistance. This will provide help to them along with feelings of value and understanding for them.

The second key for cohesion would be for you to promote trust. For a team to be cohesive at all, the members must trust one another. Encouraging employees to develop relationships that extend beyond the workplace, and giving them the opportunities to create bonds with one another will, allow them to work together as a group. They will trust and value each of their individual expertise, and work together in harmony. Conducting team building exercises and working to promote workplace unity will radically improve the degree to which your employees can work cooperatively together. This will bolster your productivity levels.

The third major key for cohesion is for you to encourage feedback amongst the team. It is much easier to work as a team when you trust in and enjoy the company of one another. Leaders and team managers can promote the development of cohesion by encouraging their people to give feedback on what is working and what is not. If your team can learn through the feedback that is being given and received, they can act quickly to keep themselves and their teammates functioning like a well–oiled machine. Constructive criticism can be your best friend as a leader, if you can manage to apply it in a positive manner.

The fourth key for cohesion is something that, you may already have naturally: healthy competition. By this I do not mean that you should necessarily elicit competition, as doing this could potentially backfire. But encouraging healthy and friendly competition amongst the team can be used as a way to promote and encourage growth. Competition makes many people better, and practicing it in a positive manner will make your team better as well. The idea of competition alone will generate the energy to motivate your people to push themselves to win. Even for those who may not necessarily win the competition, they may still use the concept to continue to grow and become better than they were before.

The final key for cohesion would be knowing how to handle the situation in cases of conflict. You can blame it on a number of reasons, but sometimes employees just do not mesh. As a result, conflict will arise. This type of friction can often make your workplace feel like a war zone. The tension and hostile environment can make the workplace uncomfortable, not just for the employees involved, but for the others around them as well. When conflict erupts, it can have a dramatic effect on productivity. Some conflict, like simple competition, will help. On the contrary, other conflict can lead to your productivity plummeting. It is important to note that, as a leader, you cannot expect to have a sterile environment all of the time. Knowing this is essential to your success and the key to earning influence. You are going to have to realize that there will be riffs and disputes among your team members, and it falls on you to be in charge of the clean–up process.

The Bible says:

"Blessed are the peacemakers, for they will be called children of God."

Become a leader of peace by opening the channels of communication and resolution. Open communication and lending a sympathetic ear to all parties involved does wonders to remedy conflict in a constructive way. Communication is everything when it comes to finding a resolution. The individuals on your team must learn to manage conflict in order to harness and improve the team's potential. When open communication occurs, it inspires team members to be part of a larger purpose, motivating each person toward trying to resolve their problems.

Your role in opening communication during times of conflict is more than just a listening ear. I recommend taking the time to point out the differences in each individual's ability to understand. Then, act as an interpreter and mediator. Most problems will stem from a simple misunderstanding, so figure out a way to speak their language, and you will be amazed by the steadfast results and unity to follow.

There will be times when resolution will seem impossible, and you may have to make an unpopular decision. This has happened to me on numerous occasions over the course of my career. The most important thing that I have taken away from these instances is that, when making an unpopular decision, it is more important to have character and stand on principle, than it is to have popularity and stand on charisma.

Do what you must to be the sounding board of reason. Be the interpreter and the peacemaker of your organization when you are faced with conflict and unpopular decisions. Much of your company culture is based on how everyone interacts with one another. A culture of respectful communication is a "top down" proposition. Business owners, directors, managers, and other supervisors set the tone for interaction in the workplace. By speaking to your employees in an honest and respectful manner, you create an environment that values integrity and communication. When you are open and honest, employees are more likely to follow suit.

As a company gets larger, there can be a tendency for the "institution" to dampen the "inspiration." As a leader, it is important to keep this from happening at all costs. There are always going to be days where inspiration will be lacking. However, allowing the institution mindset to infiltrate your organization walls and your employees' mindsets should never occur. Prevent this by remaining inspired and continuing to share the inspiration with others.

Acknowledge your team's strengths, and openly appreciate the energy they bring to a certain task. Take notice of their achievements. When inspiration seems to be lacking, roll up your sleeves and get involved! You cannot lead from an ivory throne and expect to inspire those who surround you. Your team wants to know that you are not afraid of getting your hands dirty. They need to be able to see your involvement so that they can continue to chase after the company's common values and follow your leadership with due diligence.

One way that I show my sales team how to do something is to get in there and make calls with them! There is nothing like joining your team and working through the challenges that they face on a daily basis together. I personally make sure to spend at least one day a week doing this, no matter how much that I have on my plate at the time. Not only does this pay off professionally, it pays off spiritually! Every day that I spend in the room with my sales team, I find myself rejuvenated with passion at the close of the day. My persistence to meet my goals is heightened, and I feel as if I am 'back in the game." You see, work will always be work but there is a difference between leaving the office tired and frustrated. Whether or not the sales team and I meet our daily goals for that day, when I join them on the sales floor, I find myself feeling more accomplished and better about what lies ahead.

Practicing self–care is an important job for everyone but especially for those in leadership positions. How can you effectively help those on your team if you aren't helping yourself first? You cannot pour from an empty cup, so you have to make sure that you take the time out to recharge, refresh, and refill! So how do you do it? You have to make the time for it; it's as simple as that.

Taking care of myself ensures that I will continue to grow and develop myself as a leader. It will also provide me with the time to reflect and plan out the daily decisions that must be made on behalf of myself, my family, my company, and my employees. Taking care of others and leading them can be tiresome. If you're taking care of yourself in the process, however, then you will find it to be much more rewarding than it is draining.

I encourage you to find something that helps you build upon your leadership strengths while also allowing you the outlet necessary to practice a healthy amount of self–care. For me, it is reading the Bible. Every day I wake up early to read my Bible. I allow the Living Word to challenge me both mentally as well as spiritually. This benefits my mind and my spirit, allowing me to create a roadmap of the challenges that lie ahead of me for that day.

No matter your personal definition of self–care, it should involve a deep practice of tuning in, tuning out, and being honest with yourself and those on your team. Great leaders know that they may face challenges to their decisions. In fact, it is almost inevitable. But they can also recognize these challenges and react accordingly. By doing this, you will be that much more inspiring to their team, as they will be leading from an authentic sense of purpose and vision.

"Two are better than one, because they have a good reward for their toil" – Ecclesiastes 4:9

CHAPTER 4

Changing and Transforming

"The secret of change is to focus all of your energy not on fighting the old, but on building the new." – Socrates

Change is a constant part of life. It is something that is quite simply unavoidable. As leaders, it is entirely on us to embrace change, as well as to view it as an opportunity for growth. Your team most likely will not see it in that light, at least not at first. Our influence as leaders, however, will have the potential to impact how easily (or difficult) that change will occur within our organization. To do this, we must first understand ourselves. Know that change will be measured by its impact on all who are connected to it. Based on my own personal failures (as well as my successes as a manager), I believe that all great leaders possess many similar qualities.

Great leaders seem to possess an understanding of their own behaviors. This discipline, once it has become a habit, will allow us to reference our own experiences and challenges. It leads to effective changes. We can think back on how we would probably behave in the given situation in order to better lead our team during times of transformation.

Another quality that great leaders will have is an understanding of their own actions. To be aware means that we can interpret what drives the way we act. What reasoning is behind our actions in certain situations? Are we level–headed or do we have a short temper? Do we tend to get frustrated or stressed out quicker then the average person, or can we hold on and stay calm in stressful situations? These are questions that great leaders can be honest and answer, as well as know how to control. This brings me to yet another quality that great leaders seem to possess.

Leaders have an understanding of their own thoughts and feelings. I have discovered through the years that, by understanding my own personal thoughts and feelings, I understand who I am as a person. When you are self–aware, you gain the ability to sympathize with those who are around you. As a leader, having this ability is absolutely priceless.

Great leaders have what I like to call authenticity in their communication. Authenticity is key. We cannot lead someone in a truly genuine way if we do not even believe it in ourselves. To sell yourself, you must be sold on yourself. I do not mean arrogant, but you have to be confident. When we are casting a vision or idea of change, we must be sold. When you are telling others the great direction that we as a team are going to be heading into, it requires the buy–in and effort of your team. For this reason, we must be sure that we are leading from our heart and not just our lips. Do not be afraid to show vulnerability to your team. Vulnerability is the birthplace of authenticity. Authenticity cannot be faked; it has to be honest. You have to be viewed upon as trustworthy.

Personally, my team's communication style seems to come to life when we approach communication as a collaborative relationship–driven process, rather than a top–down announcement or memo–style approach. It is important to involve your team in conversations regarding change. During these times, there are several things we, as "change leaders" must keep in mind. We want to increase team involvement and team enthusiasm within our organizations. A change leader is defined by the

American Management Association as a leader who uses their ability to influence and enthuse others through such actions and ideas as personal advocacy, vision, and drive, while facilitating change. A change leader can use a variety of processes in order to assist with the transition during times of change. For one, us leaders should be sure to spare no detail. Often people will bring up the phrase "less is best." This is not one of those occasions. In times where we are explaining the processes to our team, more is best. You must take care to explain everything in detail! We, as leaders, may think that we are doing our team members a favor by withholding certain details or aspects of how we plan to get to where we are going. More often than not, however, those we lead may view the lack of details as poor planning, uncertainty, and/or disorganization. Their assumptions can lead to discouragement amongst the group. Therefore, it is extremely important to keep them in the loop in a timely and informative manner. In these situations, it is okay to give full disclosure and to be transparent in your actions. In fact, it is preferred.

A change leader must also understand the concerns of their team. We can easily forget that those we manage might very well feel overwhelmed at the sheer volume of ideas which get discussed in planning meetings. My solution is to anticipate this and be sensitive to the fact that change can (and will) evoke fear if it is not properly communicated and managed. We must "feel their fears," if you will, and try our best to stay ahead of a possible catastrophe before it occurs. We also should take care to not perceive silence as acceptance. If things become quiet in the planning meeting, that is when your ears should be perking up! It is easy to recognize people who are not on board when they voice their concerns. In the 20+ years of which I have led others professionally, I have learned that those who say nothing can bring momentum to a screeching halt. The most effective way to prevent this is through effective and open communication and collaboration. In many cases, this will help you. I have had team members come up with some brilliant ideas for our company on their own on several occasions. Regardless as to what ideas they may come up with, people enjoy feeling like they have been invited to being a part of the process, and if we have an open collaborative environment, they will be more apt to get on board, even if their idea is not the one that ends up being chosen. Silence can often be someone's loudest scream. You must take care to listen out for it.

Know that this works both ways. I used to think that I was a pretty good communicator myself, until I was in an open leadership meeting and decided to ask my team for complete honesty and transparency! What I had originally viewed as effective communication was nothing more than me telling everyone else what I wanted to see and expected to happen. True communication is a two-way street, not a monologue. When it is done correctly, communication will result in powerful and engaging conversations. Only when conversation becomes a habit will we see the type of seamless communication that we as leaders often dream of.

While we are discussing the idea of two-way communication, we should discuss technology as well. Do not favor technology over face-to-face communication. Not in the workplace or at home. I love technology as much as anyone else. Technology fits the idea of change, as it is constantly transforming and evolving. That being said, I have learned that when it comes to leading change, your own people skills will go a long way. The latest technological breakthroughs of our time have allowed our industry to advance faster than we ever could have imagined, but people have remained the same. If you want to see positive, effective growth, then you must learn how to improve your face-to-face people skills. Get inside your team's head. Find out what motivates them and what discourages them. Learn what makes them tick, ask them what their own personal goals are and where they see themselves in relation to where your organization is going. This will ignite a passion on the inside of them to go head-to-head with change. This passion that will live inside of them is something that no amount of money can buy, and nothing can be substituted in place of.

After these processes, you have one last thing left for you to do as a leader: show your gratitude and your appreciation. This one is simple, easy, and goes a very long way. Simply put, when people around you do their job well, and help to benefit the team as a group, let me know how much you appreciate it. Let them know how important they are to your dream. Every person in your place of business is important, from the CEO to the person who changes the lightbulbs. In my experience, affirmation builds a person up like nothing else will, and it will encourage your team to keep up the good work because they WANT to, rather than because they are told that they HAVE to.

There are many ways to do this. A simple comment when you walk by their desk on how excited you are and happy with them does it. We, in the past, have catered in lunch after our team has accomplished a major feat. Occasionally we will hand out gift cards or bring in coffee and donuts. Many times, I do not actually tell them that I plan on doing this until last minute. This will surprise your fellow workers, and can create a bond between every member of the company. Change can be difficult. Acknowledge that to them. Let them know that it is difficult for you as well, because it is entirely true. Change can take a great toll on even the most experienced of leaders. Yet, if we lead from a place of understanding and keep our team informed of strategy and policy shifts as they happen, we will emerge as a stronger team because of it. We will be more apt to navigate the ever-changing waters of the business with excitement and determination. Companies change; there is no doubt about it. If you, as a leader, are willing to do a bit of homework, trust in the team that you have set out in front of you, as well as be sure to guide that team, then together you can make any team a successful one.

Despite the benefits that can often come as a result of change, change is often misunderstood. Organizations can all too often become hijacked themselves when trying to control or manage change. As leaders, we must be careful and make sure to avoid this. Like I have mentioned previously, we must be clear in our communications. There are a few effective ways to go about this.

For one, we must be leaders of integrity. We must be sure to stick to our morals and ideals even when the path to do so proves to be difficult to follow. We set the example in the face of change. We, as leaders, should show our dedication. In order to show this effectively, we must spend time and energy on a task until it is completely finished.

Another aspect that strong leaders need to possess in times of change would be nobility. You should be a humble individual who is gracious in both defeat as well as victory. You should retain your dignity in times where you are wrong, and allow others to retain theirs when you are correct in a disagreement. We also should make sure to have humility. Everyone is important in making the vision a reality. No one is superior or inferior to any other person. A humble leader recognizes this, not by putting themselves down in front of their team, but by acknowledging that all individuals of the team are equal in value, regardless of their positions within the company.

Yet, another key technique and trait that leaders should take into consideration would be openness. Being open to a variety of ideas and tactics that will come from your team will allow you to take a step back and make the decision that is better for the team and company as a whole. An open leader listens to their people without shutting them down or writing them off before they finish what they are sharing. In the uncertain world of new territory, being open-minded will bring with it a plethora of benefits.

The final trait that I want to discuss here is creativity. Being creative will help you in areas where you need to think critically. By thinking outside of the box, you will be viewed upon as innovative and can come up with endless possibilities on how to bring in changes to your company. Ideas lead to actions. Actions can lead to successes. With your own creativity, as well as the creativity of your team, you all can work on changes and create changes of your own that everyone else would understand and agree with. Creativity is not something that I believe can be taught. However, everyone is creative in some form or another, and it is up to you as a leader of change to find out what to do with the creativity that you have placed in front of you in order to best facilitate change amongst the team.

Change itself can come in many different forms and sizes. Change can take the place of beloved employees leaving, new employees starting, promotions, or simply changes in long–time policies. Change could additionally come to the product that your business sells, or the tactics that the industry of which you are in could be shifting. People, and places are subject to change at any moment's notice. Change is often brought on by the discovery of new ideas and goals. Change should be used to help your team reach these ideas and goals. This falls entirely on how you as a leader will express the change to your team. If it is presented in a poor lighting, it will be received poorly. It is up to you to meet change head-on, and cooperate with your team to better prepare for it.

One historic leader who understood the importance of change was a man named Henry Ford, whom many know was the founder of the Ford Motor Company. Likewise, he was one of the sponsors of the assembly line technique. The assembly line technique led to the mass production of automobiles, and is used by nearly every major automobile manufacturer. Before Ford Motor Company, automobiles were built by hand. This was a long and costly process. The vast majority of Americans simply could not afford to purchase automobiles. Henry Ford saw an opportunity for change, both for the nation as well as for his own company. Through use of his assembly line, production of an automobile went from twelve hours to just two and a half hours. This also greatly reduced the price tag on Ford's vehicles, which is something that he was looking to constantly improve. While America's cars were only purchased by the wealthy at the time, Ford saw a nation in which we were mobile. While other companies catered to the rich, Henry Ford and Ford Motor Company were looking to reach the masses. Henry Ford's first mass produced vehicle, the Model T, sold off of the line with an original price tag of $850. A few years later, prices for the Model T dropped to as low as $260, while Ford continued to improve the vehicle with new safety features, more reliability, as well as improved speed. Henry Ford successfully created a better automobile that was also cheaper than any other vehicle of its time. But creating better cars was not the only thing that Henry Ford changed in his time.

In January 1914, Henry Ford had made a public announcement to increase the wages of his factory workers to five dollars per day for an eight-hour shift. This was over double the amount average factory workers were paid for what was normally a nine-hour shift. By today's standards, it would roughly equate to about $120 per day!

This was done for several reasons. For one, Ford knew that this would greatly decrease what was a fairly high turnover rate for his company. Workers would be happy and easily able to care for their family. What were once disgruntled employees were now beginning to work with joy and excitement. This also led to people lining up outside of his factories in search of a job in the factories. Productivity went through the roof. In a matter of a couple of years, profit nearly doubled. By paying employees more, he ended up cutting his costs and increased his profit. He also had a newfound group of consumers, as workers in his factory would now be able to purchase the vehicles that they helped to build!

This change led to a stronger company and a happier team overall. This also led to extreme pressure to the growing competitors in the industry, who were either refusing to or otherwise unable to match the wages that Henry Ford was able to. By changing what the rest of his competitors had simply conformed to, Henry Ford strengthened his business and his team, not only by numbers but by quality of labor. Henry himself was one of the earliest innovators and change leaders in his respected industry. His story is one of fame and success as a direct result to the changes that he was able to create as well as embrace. Needless to say, change is important. Change can be your best friend as a leader if you are able to embrace it and share it properly amongst your team.

I believe that not only is change a part of life, but it is a necessity for any person, especially one who is in a leadership position. Famed martial artist Bruce Lee was in an interview and famously said that one should "be like water." What I believe he meant by that statement is that you should always be adapting to a world that is ever-changing. Being stagnant for too long has never lead to success. A stagnant body of water only creates algae, while water that is constantly flowing will generate power. Just as a river is in motion at all times, we should be moving and transforming at all times in our individual areas of expertise. By that same token, an acorn needs a lot of change before it can become a tree. An infant will crawl before they start to walk, and walk before they are able to run. These dreams all become a reality through change. Change is found in anyplace that you look. At 99 degrees Celsius, water is hot.

But at 100 degrees Celsius, water boils. Change. God uses change in many times in our own lives in order to teach us.

Remember my infamous construction job that I mentioned? Remember how I mentioned that I detested the job and often would not show up? Well, that David needed a change. He needed a transformation. In his scenery. His way of thinking. His approach (or lack thereof) towards reaching his actual passion. Today's David Villa is much different from the David Villa who was calling out "sick" and not going to work every other day. I had to make a change. I had to get hungrier. I had to get to where my vision was no longer simply a vision. The major difference between that point in my life and today, was change. This change was on a large scale, and it took a lot out of me to do it. I had to completely transform my own way of thinking in order to get out of that point. To quote Robert Frost, I decided to take the proverbial road less traveled, and that made all the difference. The road to change was not one that was easy. It wasn't paved. There were cracks and bumps and many obstacles that I would stumble over. That is the thing about change. There are not many changes that are easy, even those that seem to be on a small scale. Often, to deviate from what you know is to go against your natural makeup. Humans are not always so quick to be able to change our daily habits. But sometimes habits need to be broken for us to better our chances of success. If you have been utilizing a specific tactic that fails each and every time, you need to change it! Doing what is easiest is not always the best. The quickest answer that comes to mind is not always the correct answer. Using the least amount of effort will almost certainly fail. You need to have an open mind. You need to be innovative. You need to be creative. For these traits and techniques, you need to change.

One leader who could be called the face of change would be the brilliant inventor known as Nikola Tesla. Nikola Tesla saw the world not for what it was, but for what it could be with a few changes. His contributions, specifically his electrical engineering work with what is known as alternating current, helped to shape many aspects of the world that we know today. His changes and ideas were often viewed as insane and impossible visions for his time period, but Tesla knew better.

In much of the 1800s, consumers relied on what is known as direct current (DC)–based electricity. Direct current was very unreliable at the time and could not reach very great lengths. It was an expensive and inefficient resource. Because of this, Nikola Tesla devoted much of his life to study electrical engineering. He developed a way to harness the power of alternating current, or AC, which was a much more efficient and cheaper source of electricity for the public. Tesla believed that electricity should be something that is cheap and readily available for everyone. Today, Tesla's alternating current is used to power houses, office buildings, and other large buildings. This is something that would be nearly impossible and potentially dangerous to do with a direct current.

Nikola Tesla saw a chance for change and a shot at creating a better life for himself and those around him, and he took the chance. He wanted to be the change that he felt the world needed. Nikola worked tirelessly and would often go without sleep in order to work on his product. His invention is felt today, and the work he accomplished within his specific field of study. Elon Musk's company, Tesla Motors, is in fact named after Nikola Tesla to pay homage to the great inventor's work with electricity. In fact, the Tesla Roadster that was first released in 2008 uses an alternating current battery in part due to the work that Nikola Tesla started back in the 1880s! Nikola Tesla's work, changes, and contributions were clearly ahead of its time.

This, again–like many other great innovations–required changes before they were to become a reality. There was a process involved before Tesla could push his product out into the world, just as there will be a process of change in order for us as leaders to become more efficient in what we do. You have to be there to make sure the transition in times of change goes smoothly.

Change will happen. In your industry. In your business. In your office building. In your relationships. Maybe even in your own dreams and vision. But hear me when I say that it is completely okay. Expect change, because like it or not, it will come. When change finally arrives, embrace it with your arms outreached. If you take care and are prepared for it, your team will follow in your footsteps, ready to great change as it arrives. Change is necessary, and in many cases, change is needed.

"My flesh and my heart may fail, but God is the strength of my heart and my portion forever" – Psalms 73:26

CHAPTER FIVE

Being Yourself but Your Best Self

"Always be yourself. Express yourself. Have faith in yourself. Do not go out and look for a successful personality and duplicate it." – Bruce Lee

It is common knowledge that different people have different strengths and weaknesses. That much is certain. Using your strengths, as well as your originality to your advantage, is something that is not only beneficial. It is absolutely necessary in your journey to being a successful leader. But what do we do with that information? We must internalize and then utilize that concept within ourselves. Rather than try to change our personality to fit others around us, we should take what makes us good at what we do, add a few tweaks and changes, and become great. You have the ability within YOU to be successful. What works for others may not work for you, and what you find to be beneficial may in turn prove to be harmful to those who are following in your footsteps. In a leadership position, the idea of "fake it until you make it" will simply fail. People can feel when someone is not whole-heartedly involved. You must be you, plain and simple. You must also be your best you. You must be someone who captivates others, draws them to you, coaches them, points them in the right direction, and shares their successes as well as shortcomings, all while being yourself. By standing out, you will draw attention and others around you will follow. By using your strengths and your passions in order to lead others, you will flourish.

I learned many years ago how important using your strengths and originality is in the workplace. For those who know me, this story may come as a bit of a shock. Many years ago, I was down on my luck. I was in desperate need of some steady income. I was twenty years old, had recently married and became a new father. I was a kid in one hand, still trying to find what it was that I really wanted to do with my life. I was a man in the other, with a wife and child to worry about. The bills were piling up, and I needed to find something to do, fast! The father of an old friend of mine suggested that I work with him. He was a vice president of a construction unit, and told me that I could become quite successful if I kept up with the job. It was a union job, involving hard work. It was very demanding and tiring. Although it was not my passion, it would pay the bills for the time being. So, I agreed, and later joined a union. The job consisted of hard physical labor, bending pipes and hooking up electrical wires together and whatnot.

In case you can't tell by reading this, I had no idea what I was doing! It is safe to say that I absolutely hated the job. It was not what I had envisioned at all. The other guys who were on the job sites with me knew it. To them I was lazy. I called out more days than I went in. It was an eight-month job, and in total I must have worked for about four months. But I was not lazy. There was a far larger underlying issue at hand than just common laziness. I was not passionate! It was only a job. Its function to me was to pay my bills and support my family. It served no other purpose and did nothing for me internally. This was not my dream, not all I had set out for my life and for my family. I did not want to go because it did not fulfill me. For the guys there who enjoyed that type of work, they were successful and could have become journeymen in a matter of a few years. But that was not my dream. Now, being that I had joined a union, they really did not have an easy time firing me. Instead, they would simply move me from site to site, working at various locations, proving to be effective in none of them. Technically, I am still employed there, as I merely stopped showing rather than quit! It was safe to say that the manual labor type of job was not for me.

There is a popular quote by the late motivational speaker Leo Buscaglia, who said: "The easiest thing to be in the world is you. The most difficult thing to be is what other people want you to be." Many others would probably have benefitted from me if I had the determination and interest in my job as a laborer. However, this was not what I had in mind. I knew deep down that I was different. This job may have not been my forte, but that I could find one that was. I had skills, and even when others may not have seen them, I knew that they were there. I knew that I needed to find something that put them to use. I remember being on the job sites and having other guys look at me confused, wondering how on earth that I could have possibly found myself doing this kind of work! They knew I was different as well. It did not feel good at the time to be different. It stung, until I understood how important being set aside from the rest can be.

Be genuine. Be unique. Be different.

It is completely okay to stand out amongst others. In many cases, it is preferred (except when in a construction job!) By proving yourself to be separate from the rest, people will gravitate towards you. To be able to do this is the mark of a strong leader. Instead of telling others what to do, show them how to do it. They, in turn, will have faith in you as a leader and understand that you have their best interests in mind. This is important, especially for those who have a large vision. With a large vision for your company and for your future, you will most likely need a group of people, backed by a competent leader. I like to relate this to scripture, which can show you first hand the benefits of having a strong-willed and inspiring person in a leadership position. In John 10, Jesus discusses a shepherd and his flock of sheep. He explains how the sheep know their shepherd's voice as he calls them out by name. He then leads them, walking the same path only a few steps ahead of them. The sheep will not follow a stranger's voice, only the voice of their trusted leader; the shepherd. Furthermore, the shepherd must care greatly about the sheep in order to protect and lead them in the event of a catastrophe. The shepherd comforts and protects the sheep, and in turn the sheep will trust in and care for the shepherd.

For those who haven't caught on, YOU are the shepherd and your team is your sheep. You are responsible for leading them and showing them the way. You must walk the path ahead of them, checking for every roadblock and every obstacle that you will need to show them how to overcome. You must use your own personal strengths in order to assist your workers. You must realize that you need your workers to be just as involved as you. If your vision is an oak tree and all you have is an acorn, then you will need some help! You and you alone must lead them, follow them, or get out of their way!

As I mentioned in Chapter 1, our internal theme at iPD, which is: "All In". This is as much for me as it is for every member in the company. I have spent many days side by side with my sales team, making call after call deep within the trenches with them. We, as a team, rise together, fall together, and rise again. As a leader, we should never ask someone to do something that we are not willing to do ourselves, and I try my best to live by that message. This, in itself, will set you apart from the majority. The everyday manager, barking orders and sitting back will prove to be ineffective. The boss who suggests tips and then does the opposite will not be respected. You must be different in the sense that you work alongside your team. You must be different by leading by example day in and day out, by using your strengths to benefit and uplift yourself as well as those around you. Your team will appreciate it, learn from it, and you may learn a thing or two yourself!

I have had several discussions in the past on the differences between a manager and a leader. These differences, although very subtle, can drastically change the effectiveness of what you are trying to accomplish. A manager copies, while a leader is original. While an everyday manager will be content with being like others, a leader would rather rise above normalcy and stand out amongst their peers. A manager follows set systems and structures that were previously set, while a leader is more focused on the development of people. A strong and intuitive leader knows that by building up their people, everyone flourishes. A manager relies on control, whereas a leader relies on trust. It is much more beneficial to be trusted and confided in, than to be feared and avoided. A person will bend over backwards and go above and beyond what is expected of them. They believe that their leader cares for them, respects them, and needs them. Many leaders can struggle with that important connection that needs to be made with their workers. It takes a truly special and unique leader to be able to form this bond. However, if you can manage to form this type of relationship with your team, your business will reach newfound heights in terms of both revenue as well as general relations and camaraderie within the workplace.

This all, consequently, leads back to being the best you that you can be as a leader. By being original and natural, and not coming off as artificial when speaking with your team, they will trust your character. By using your strengths while acknowledging and working on your weaknesses, you show that you are human and relate to them. By showing them the correct way to go about tasks and handle obstacles, they will trust your judgment. By working alongside them and being diligent and successful with your job, they will trust your work ethic. Thus, the team as a whole, will rise to meet the occasion. Iron sharpens iron, having a solid team around you will only benefit you. This process starts with leadership. This process, too, starts with you. It will also have a trickle–down effect in many cases, such as when you in turn promote others around you. Workers will view a manager that you have set in place as someone of great integrity and skill. Being that they know the type of individual you are, they will be more likely to accept and work effectively with those that you have put in a place of authority.

Being a leader does not mean that you have to be the best at every aspect of your job. On the contrary, most leaders will excel at maybe one or two aspects and use that strength to their advantage. A successful leader can acknowledge their shortcomings, while utilizing their good traits and talents. Take Elon Musk, for example. Elon Musk, CEO of Tesla Inc. (among other businesses) took his company and pushed it into international fame. He took his passion for science and thirst for change and never-ending questions of "what if" and shot Tesla to superstardom. Tesla's current market value is estimated to be around $48 billion, which is currently higher than Ford Motor Company. With a leader hungry for more, who uses his exceptional public speaking skills and his genuine interest in technology, they have become a household name. All of this, without spending a dime on advertising. Yes, believe it or not, Tesla relies entirely on word of mouth to sell their product, along with the energy and fame of their CEO, of course. But Elon Musk is not the only example of a leader who uses his originality and strengths to lead his business and build interest into his product.

Apple is one of the most popular and successful businesses in the world. Some have referred to Apple as "the most powerful franchise in America," and it is a difficult statement to argue against. There is a strong chance that many of you currently reading this own or have owned at least one Apple product. Apple Inc is currently worth around $800 billion. Over three quarters of a TRILLION dollars! All of this, with help from their co-founder, the late Steve Jobs.

Steve, like Elon Musk, relied on his passionate speeches about his work and projects for Apple. Whereas Elon Musk tends to inform and let his own work intrigue consumers, Steve Jobs riled up and excited consumers with his powerful discussions. He told the public of new and exciting features, of things going on behind the scenes at Apple. He was so enthralled by his work that he seemingly almost HAD to share it with someone. Steve took pleasure from seeing the look on the faces of others when he discussed the latest iPhone. He yearned to not only have his product finished, but to have it admired and adored by those who purchased it. With these keynote speeches and press conferences held by Apple and run by Jobs, the public grew to feel as if they really knew Steve, and you could tell from listening to him speak for any length of time that he was different.

Eccentric, exciting, and always pushing the envelope just a little bit further. Steve relied on his own eccentricities in order to sell himself while he described his dreams and visions. Steve, however, was not only a solid speaker but an innovative and unique leader. There is a popular and controversial story about a trip Steve Jobs had made in 1979 to a company started by Xerox, known as Palo Alto Research Company, or PARC. PARC was giving a demonstration to potential investors, Steve being one of the few who received an invitation to come. In exchange for an investment, Steve would be allowed to view some of the new products and inner workings of the company. While on the tour, one simple aspect caught Steve's attention. The computer mouse. You see, previous computers utilized a large, heavy mouse that was both unreliable as well as extremely difficult and time consuming for a user. PARC had a much simpler mouse, smaller, and easily used to navigate a personal computer. Jobs saw this, and implored his engineers to find a more cost efficient and even easier alternative. Apple created the new and improved mouse, which was both cheaper and more reliable than its counterpart. This action changed Apple, and Apple in turn, changed the world.

Yet, another leader who uses his originality would be Mark Zuckerberg. Zuckerberg, like both Musk as well as Jobs, created something from nothing. Co-founder and chairman of Facebook, Mark Zuckerberg, at 22, became the youngest billionaire in the world. He loved and believed in his company so much so that he dropped out of Harvard in order to further develop it. Mark's approach to leadership and being different is very unlike both Steve jobs and Elon Musk, however. Unlike the previous two, Mark is not known for being a very good public speaker. He can often appear awkward and uncomfortable and seems to try and shy away from the limelight when he is able to. He is more comfortable at working behind the scenes, spending his time consumed with the features and inner workings of Facebook. Facebook employees near to Zuckerberg describe him as a leader who is encouraging and aggressive with his work. He is said to love debates on the processes and ideas within the company, while demanding innovation and growth. While other leaders who have a personality for the public, Zuckerberg knows that this is not his strength and would rather rely on that which he excels at: motivating and coming up with ideas for the bettering of the company and its workers. Today Facebook is worth an estimated $435 billion. Mark has built an empire that is rivaled by no others in the ever-changing world of social media. Many other companies in various other industries rely on Facebook for its ability to reach the masses, as there are an estimated 1.23 billion active monthly users! The ability of Facebook to provide instant and easily accessed advertising is immense. All thanks to Mark Zuckerberg's leadership and ability to be constantly growing and evolving.

All three leaders that we have discussed vary greatly in terms of leadership style, their approach, and their strengths. But how do the three relate to one another? All three are successful. All three have proven to be strong leaders who have impacted their company in a positive manner. Whether you have the knowledge and love of science like Elon Musk, the great people skills of Steve Jobs, or the immense work ethic and drive to motivate your workers like Mark Zuckerberg, you must use what you are best at to be the most effect in your area of expertise.

Maybe you aren't a Zuckerberg who can form ideas and know how to properly motivate your team. Maybe you aren't a Jobs who gets up and commands attention when you are up speaking at a convention. Maybe you are not even a Musk, who seemingly knows more about his product than the others who are physically creating it. But a strong leader will find the qualities of their own that can benefit their team, and they will use them to their advantage.

How does one do this? To look inside oneself and acknowledge that you have areas of strength is to also realize that you have areas of weakness as well. It takes the power and humility to set aside ego for the greater good of your team, your company, and yourself. No one likes to point out their own faults. No one likes to accept the fact that you may not be the best in something. You may even be terrible at it! By stating that yourself, it will humble you and allow you to receive assistance from others. You cannot do everything perfectly. You can, however, do some things quite well. Use your strengths and have someone there ready to help you through your weaknesses. The first step is admitting that you have a problem!

If I could think about the top five most successful leaders in my own personal life, they would all have a couple of things in common: They use their strengths to their advantages, and they do not lead from the top–down. They lead from the inside–out. Through this, they inspire those around them. These leaders either find strength in change, or they teach themselves how to accept it. With change, a leader can choose to either manage and try to control it, or they can embrace change, and see where it can take them. You must involve the concept of change as a strength of yours, because it is inevitable. A leader who welcomes change and shows strength in the face of it will excite and influence their team to follow suit. I like to think that the absolute best work gets done when every single person in the room is excited, interested, and striving towards the same goal as one another. There are no bad ideas or stupid questions when every single person is trying to do their part and use their strengths and originality in order to better the team. This, like everything else in business, starts with the leader.

I have been told that one of my strengths would be the ability to get people excited about whatever it is that I am excited about. I often will have an idea that is so captivating to me that I absolutely have to blurt it out and discuss it with someone, and, in turn, my team has become the same! We hold meetings every so often with some of the managers of my company that we commonly refer to as "leadership meetings." In these leadership meetings, we all will bounce ideas off of one another. We discuss what is going on within our own departments, and cooperatively go over how we all can be better at what we do.

I love the various strengths and uniqueness from the individuals in those meetings. I love knowing above all else, that my dreams and visions have become their dreams and visions. They want the best for the company, and are tapping into their own personal areas of expertise in order to reach that. We have people from all walks of life in the room, all trying to accomplish the exact same task, only in different ways. These people understand the importance of standing out, as well as using their strengths in their individual day-to-day jobs. A room full of leaders who all understand these two important concepts is an enthusiastic and powerful place to be.

I like to relate this idea of using your strengths and uniqueness to sports. Often, a team or individual may win their game or match not by being the best well rounded, but by playing the game their way. By setting the pace early on and utilizing what they are best at, they can win despite being the underdog. A great example of this would be a man known as Muhammad Ali. Many know of him, but unless you are a die-hard boxing fan or have otherwise studied him, you may not know the science behind his style of boxing.

Early on in Muhammad Ali's career, he made a name for himself through his usage of his physical prowess. Ali was fast. He could throw jabs and crosses faster than most people could blink. Combining his elite level of speed with his lanky frame and wide stance, and most other boxers could not touch him. He would throw punches that stung and throw them in volume, and quickly jump or weave out of the way of his opponent. This tactic both injured other fighters as well as frustrated them greatly. Muhammad Ali knew this speed and technique was rivaled by no other in his division. This was the basis for each fight early on in Ali's career. He was a volume puncher. Instead of dropping fighters with one or two big shots, he would much rather dance around the outside of the ring, and batter his opponent through quick and persistent jabs–thanks to his speed and reach advantage.

But Ali, too, succumbed to age later in his career. Critics noticed in later fights that, although Ali could still box, he had slowed noticeably. What once was his greatest strength no longer seemed to work for him. Ali knew that he had to change his methods of fighting if he were to still compete at an elite level. His trainers mentioned to him a different style of boxing entirely that they felt would fit his needs and adhere to his newfound weaknesses.

Later on in Ali's career, he began to employ a tactic which relied less on speed and more on his own intelligence as a boxer. Rather than attempt to bob and weave between punches, he would often lean against the ropes, ducking what he could and often absorbing blows until his opponent was exhausted. This tactic did two separate things for Muhammad Ali; the elasticity of the ropes helped to absorb much of the force from the punch of the other boxer, rather than Ali's head and body taking all of the blow. This style also would quickly tire out many boxers who relied on heavy punches. Then, once the opponent was tired and worn out from swinging wildly at him, Ali would answer with counter punches. He would steadily turn up the pressure on his now tired and defenseless opponent until they succumbed to his relentless jabs and crosses. This strategy, now commonly referred to as the "rope-a-dope" technique, was created almost entirely by Muhammad Ali. He used the rope-a-dope method and fought his fight the way he knew best. It allowed him to defeat his rival George Foreman in 1974, and become champion for the third and final time in his career. Ali used this style until he retired officially in 1981. Today, this style is still widely popular amongst defensive fighters in order to minimize damage from their opponent.

The point of this story on Muhammad Ali is to show, without a doubt, the benefits of fighting with your strengths rather than your weaknesses. Many think of Ali as the boxer who was so fast that he was nearly impossible to hit. I like to also think about this slower style he adopted later, as it shows the perseverance and humility that it takes in order to accept a weakness of yours. Use your strength to cover it. As a leader, it is imperative to use your strengths. It is extremely important to use what you know best in your daily life. You will feel fulfilled, and overall be more successful in every aspect by using what you do best, and doing it. Fight your fight!

When one sets his or her fears, setbacks, hang ups, and ego aside–one can achieve greatness. Most are mediocre, some are good, few are great, and even fewer are completely brilliant at what they do. I have a firm belief that the top 10% of people within their respected areas of expertise are not necessarily more talented than the rest. They are not better in the sense that they are always naturally gifted. Instead, many are better for the sheer fact that they tap into their strengths, mix it with their own unique talents and characteristics, and have a few solid people close by to cover their weaknesses and setbacks. I can almost guarantee that the top 10% have a strong team around them to back them up. Accept that you have some weaknesses that need to be addressed but also accept the fact that you have some strengths that you need to bring out. If what you are doing does not involve your strengths, change what you are doing. Find something that involves them. Something that requires you to put your all into it, that compliments your personality and pairs well with whatever it is that you do BEST.

What I would like someone to take from this specific chapter among all else would be simple: take what you know, and USE IT. You have something to offer, and as a leader, you must show it, whatever "it" may be. God built you deliberately. None of your talents or traits are there by accident. If you know what your strengths are, utilize them. If you do not yet know what they are, that is completely okay! You have time to discover them, it is never too late to search inside yourself, find out what you are good at, and implicate it. Once you have found your strength, you must work on it. Perfect it. Take what you are good at and become phenomenal. It is important to realize and understand that if you aren't growing your strength than it is dying. If you aren't building up and training your strengths, then you can easily lose them. Remember like we discussed previously that it is okay to not see yourself in Steve Jobs.

It's okay to not find similarities in your style and the style of Elon Musk. It is perfectly okay to not have the education or background of Mark Zuckerberg. You are your own person and you have your own talents and skills and abilities that these guys do not have either! You must be constantly working on and developing your talents in order to achieve greatness as a leader. It is a humbling experience for your team and those who you are in charge of to see you yourself working on and training yourself to be a better you. Remember to be unique, to stick out, and be different. Be unlike any other. I believe that the word "weird" is just a word that boring people use to describe people who are unique. Be yourself, but be your best self.

Ephesians 2:10 For we are God's handiwork, created in Christ Jesus to do good works, which God prepared in advance for us to do.

CHAPTER SIX

Fueled by Failure

"Failure is an event, not a person. Yesterday ended last night."
– Zig Ziglar

Failure. To fail. To try something in the hopes of being victorious and to come up short. We, as leaders, cannot afford to waste time and energy by obsessing over failure. Failure can be your greatest motivation or your biggest discouragement. To be afraid of failure will cripple you. It can be a major roadblock, not only in your work but in your life. In previous chapters, we discussed the concept of having to take action and get out of a rut in order to do this. I previously told the story of my children learning to swim and to jump into the pool. The fear of them failing once they hit the water froze them where they stood. The idea that something bad may happen, or that they could not do it caused them to stand at the edge, peering into the water while staring back at me. The issue is not about being afraid, that part comes with being human. The issue would be if they had stayed paralyzed by failure. This paralysis can happen on a much larger scale as well.

When starting iPD, I was young and still wet behind the ears. I had a lot of maturing to do and a lot of knowledge that needed to be attained before I could make my dreams and vision a reality. Failure is something for which I could probably write two thousand chapters. I have failed time and time again in my own life, to put it mildly. There have been many occasions in which things did not turn out the way I had planned. I am human and in a position now that I can look back on these times, acknowledge them with a laugh, and move on. But nothing about my journey was easy. Even today, failure is still an option. Failure is always an option. In fact, failure is usually the easiest option available! Failure is understandable and forgivable. Not even trying, however, is not. I want to discuss why it is okay to fail, and how we can actually use failure as a huge motivator rather than something that discourages us.

If you have ever attempted anything at all that was worth attempting, chances are that you have experienced some level of failure. It may be on a small scale, such as failing a test in grade school, or a larger scale–like having your own business collapse. You have experienced some sort of failure. Failure is tough. Failure is painful. There is nothing fun about it; it hurts your pride and can hurt your bank account. But it is necessary. Failure humbles the arrogant, teaches the oblivious and naïve, and strengthens the optimist. What I mean by that is this: those with a positive attitude can come to know failure as their greatest teacher. In some cases, failure can be beneficial later on down the road. CEO and chairman of Disney Corporation, Michael Eisner, has said that failure is good–as long as you do not make a habit out of it. You must respect and understand that there is a possibility that you will fail. You must also understand that failure is not the end of the world. You can always retry. There is always time to start over and try again.

There are many now-famous tales of failure. Many have heard the story of Michael Jordan being cut from his basketball team as a young kid, or Walt Disney being fired from his news station for "lacking imagination," among other things. These stories, now almost comical to think about, were catalysts in the lives of both of these individuals path to success. If Jordan had not felt angry and determined as a result of his high school coach snubbing him, who knows if he would have really tapped into his full potential. If Walt Disney stayed and lived an ordinary life at the news station, perhaps he would not have had the opportunity to change the world through his brilliant imagination. I have also listed some of the trials and tribulations of Abraham Lincoln in previous chapters, who failed more times than he succeeded and yet managed to change his entire nation for the better.

Some other examples of failure would be Albert Einstein, who did not speak until he was four years old. His teacher told his parents that he most likely would never amount to much. At an early age, Einstein was written off as unintelligent. He had major issues with communication, was described as a "slow learner" who could not seem to grasp even the most remedial of concepts while classmates seemed to excel with ease. Albert Einstein was no child prodigy by any standards. Yet he, too, achieved greatness in his specific field. In fact, the term Einstein alone is now synonymous with the term "genius." Bill Gates dropped out of Harvard, and is now the richest man in the world. But did you know that his first business failed? What about Mark Zuckerberg, who we discussed in the previous chapter? Remember him? He made the decision to drop out of Harvard. Or take Steve Jobs, who did not quit but instead was essentially kicked out of Apple, his own business, before coming back to the company years later. What if he had decided to be bitter and not come back to the company, where would Apple be today?

All of these leaders experienced great shortcomings, ones that could have crippled them. They had weaknesses at the time. They experienced failure. Yet, when we talk about these people, we do not think of failure or of shortcomings. But they were there. I think anyone who is great has failed miserably in the past. Those feelings of defeat and dejection are natural. It is what you do afterwards that will set you apart. Do you feel pity on yourself? Do you sit and pout? Do you get angry and flustered and give up? Or do you get back up, dust yourself off, put your emotions aside, and try again? These are the questions you need to ask yourself. You must retrain your own thought process and frame of thinking and accept failure as something that is inevitably going to occur. It will be the best teacher that you will ever have. I firmly believe that you learn more from failing than you could ever learn from succeeding. I also believe that success itself would not feel as sweet without the concept and often strong possibility of failure.

On another note, failure can also weed out what you really do not care about in life. Think about it: If one failure is all it takes for you to give something up completely, it could very well be God telling you that this is not what you are meant to do. If failure just shakes you to the point to where you want to give up, maybe you are not actually following your dream. Motivational speaker Dr. Eric Thomas said something once that really stuck with me. He simply said that your WHY has to be greater than any resistance you are facing. What he meant by that statement is that your reasoning and your motivation behind what you are doing has to be larger than any possible opposition. You have to constantly be hungry. You must want success more than anything else. In order to be able to do this, your visions and your dreams have to be big. You have to really want it. If they keep you up at night, and you obsess over your dream, then a little bit of failure should not discourage you. Resistance should be expected. You must aim to succeed. Know that if you happen to be unsuccessful, that it will be okay. You will be ready to try again when all is said and done. This, for some, will be the most difficult aspect of being a leader. In a leadership position, this is especially important. You will be the comforter of your team, and failures cannot deter you or cause you to unravel, especially in front of your people. You have to be strong even when being strong is the hardest thing to do. A strong leader will be the guiding light for a team. As a leader, others will be looking towards you in times of hardship, studying your reactions and internalizing the way you handle the stress. You must take care to not frighten or discourage them during these times. In order to stay afloat, you will need everyone focused and motivated during these times. This can be the difference between a minor inconvenience and a complete and utter catastrophe that permeates through your company.

Maybe you are reading this and you are thinking to yourself: *"I can't help it. Failure is a constant occurrence for me. It's tough to not be discouraged by all of these things going on in my life."* I understand, believe me–I really do. Car repossessions, getting down to the last few dollars in your bank account, worrying about paying rent, getting groceries, having your latest business adventure take a dive. I started iPD back in 1994 and it was only within the last few years that I have truly been able to enjoy the fruitions of my labor. It has been a long journey. So yes, I've been there–I've done that.

Nothing about a leadership position is easy. Failure can make such common daily tasks like getting up and getting ready for work difficult. But understand that before Lincoln won the election on November 6th, 1860, that many probably thought he was a failure. Understand that those people who made the decision to fire Walt Disney for his "lack of imagination" probably viewed the man as a failure. Understand, that when Steve Jobs was fired and removed from the company of which he helped to start, it was because many thought of him as a failure. These successful and powerful leaders were all at one point viewed as losers.

Also take note that failure is always a possibility, as some experienced it early on in their life. Others felt the sting of failure years after they had already been established. History, as it turned out, proved their critics wrong. Time will reward you for your persistence, as long as you make the decision to be persistent. They say that God works in mysterious ways, and that is something that I whole-heartedly believe in. He will take you on a winding road, going around corners, climbing up the tallest mountains right after you finish journeying through the lowest valleys. One door closes and another door opens. Things seem to fall apart at the exact same time that other pieces seem to come together. Sometimes it is difficult to understand the predicament that you are in, especially after a major setback such as failure. But understand that you will make it out of the hole that you are in, and that you will come out stronger than you were when you went in. It isn't easy–it isn't fun–but it is possible.

There is a direct relation between leadership and failure. When something goes wrong, the first place that will be analyzed is management. This is the number one reason for success in a business, as well as failure. For the leaders reading this, that is YOU! You will receive the brunt of the judgment as a leader. This goes with the territory. Any form of failure, whether on a large scale or something insignificant, will be put on your back. You must be able to push through it. You must be able to handle that level of pressure without cracking, for the sake of your team and ultimately for the sake of yourself.

Stress is the cousin of failure. Self-doubt, self-pity, and lack of direction are also in relation. You must be able to distance yourself as much as possible from these ways of thinking, while being able to fight off and handle them when they come to you. Being a leader will test your mind. It will leave you emotionally exhausted some days. But God never puts anything on you that is too much for you to handle. No burden will be easy, but no burden will ever be too much for you to carry, either. If where you are at his hard, and you are not happy with what is going on for you right now, then you need to push past it! The enemy of failure is motivation and willpower. If your motivation is so strong that it is all you can see, then success is nearly guaranteed. Do not lose focus, do not stop working diligently, and if failure still comes your way, do not be discouraged. Let your failures fuel your successes. If you can manage to master that tactic and transform yourself into that frame of thinking, your team will follow your lead and not be discouraged in the face of adversity.

As a result, you and your team will reach newfound heights. I liken this to a fully loaded train that is traveling at top speed. Nothing short of a miracle will be able to bring that train to a complete stop. The train simply has too much power and too much force to be held back. Wind resistance, friction on the track, obstacles in the path on the train, none of these outside forces will have much effect once the train is in motion. We must view failures and negative thinking as those outside forces. If we keep on pushing at full throttle and do not concern ourselves with the things that do nothing else but harm and distract us, we will be successful in whatever industry that we specialize in. We will be better leaders. We will be better parents. We will be better spouses. We will be better people.

I believe that failure is feared and misunderstood for multiple reasons, one of which being that (as humans) we, do not like to have to face that we may have not done something correctly. This is why you will often come across an individual who does not take constructive criticism very well. You may justify in your head as to why you were right, or you will simply decide to ignore the critique altogether. Criticism, no matter how well intended, is essentially one person telling you that you are incorrect. In our heads, it can be viewed as a failure on a small scale. Just as any other failure, criticism should be taken not as a moment for discouragement, but as a moment for improvement. When a weakness or failure of yours is pointed out, accept it as an opportunity for you to learn from.

In the last chapter, we discussed the importance of strengths. But by also understanding our weaknesses, failures and short-comings, we will be better equipped to be a strong and wise leader. In the same way that you should never let success get to your head, you also should be careful to not let failures get to your heart. If I had allowed my failures and setbacks get to me, I would have quit in the first year I started iPD. You would not be holding this book in your hands. You do not have time for disappointment. You have no time for being discouraged. You cannot waste your energy on being frustrated and putting your-self down. Uplift yourself, and you will uplift others around you. Use your failures and past issues as a testimony for all who care to listen. You, as a leader, can inspire your team with your story. Everybody loves the underdog. Everyone loves the story of the one who should not have succeeded but somehow managed to do so. I have the testimony. The leaders that we spoke of previously have that story. Chances are, you have a testimony of your own as well. Your own personal testimony can be your best tool when discussing the concept of failure. Use your failures to relate to others around you. Forming a bond through this with your team is something that will be very valuable to you, and to them as well.

It takes a special type of person to be able to do this. To be a leader who can stare in the face of potential failure and adver-sary and stay positive for the sake of their workers will test you. It will take patience, as well as an individual who is men-tally tough. You must develop thick skin, and not outwardly show that you are flustered or panicking, even when you are! You must try your hardest to not take this stress out on anyone. Instead, take it out on your work. Work extra diligently and be sure to stay the course. Remember that everyone who is doing something innovative goes through some trials and tribulations. Smooth seas do not make good sailors; you will most likely fail again and again. But then, by being persistent and staying on task, you will start to succeed. I can only imagine the amount of people who could have changed the world and their area of expertise if they had not given up. To look back and see just how far you could have gone, or what person you could have been, if you had not quit and kept moving forward. Rather than sit and wonder what you would have done if you had not let failure win, go out there and find out!

I experienced firsthand how difficult this process can be, and what kind of toll it can take on you. In 2008, business was not doing well, to say the least. Our nation was in an economic decline, and the automotive industry upon which I am involved in and rely on, took a hit. We, as a country, were in one of the lowest economic time periods since the Great Depression. This time, now known as the Great Recession, was nearly fatal to iPD. Our customers were frustrated. Our product was taking a beating from several different outside forces, and there really wasn't much that we could do.

In a matter of thirty days, I lost nearly every member of my sales team. I had nearly accepted failure as my own destiny. It almost certainly would have been easier to just get up from my desk, wipe my hands clean of this responsibility, and went on to go out and get a normal nine-to-five job. Everything that could have gone wrong at the time period did. But I had other people to worry about. My family were the few people left who were employees of mine. I owed it to these people as a father, a spouse, and a leader, to try to pull us out of this mess that we were in. I made the decision to try in the face of nearly certain failure and it made all the difference. We bunkered down, and busted our tail. We made things happen. We had to create something out of nothing. It was not easy by any standards.

In fact, 2008 reminded me very much of what it felt like when the company was first started. The little dream that I had in 1994 that became a massive dream that in turn became a reality. The livelihood of my team and I. The company that was just starting to impact the industry in a big way had started to slip from me. My dream nearly died that year. However, God had bigger plans for it. By ignoring the voice of doubt and failure, we survived 2008. We were damaged, and felt the sting of that year for a long time after, but we survived.

It took me about three years before I felt like I was in a position to fully recruit an entire sales team. Once we were whole again, we went right back to building ourselves back from the ground up. Things changed since then. We went at things with a little more hunger. A little more determination. I got a little taste of what could have happened, and I did not like it one bit. I myself would not go back to where I was, nor would I be coming into the office one day to sit my employees down and thank them for the long ride. I, and we, were in this together and for the long haul.

Some days the concept of failure during that time was almost music to my ears. The idea of waking up without the stress and hustle and bustle for a little while sounded almost pleasant. I am very grateful and I count my lucky stars that I did not fall into that trap. Complacency would have certainly lead to failure, and only the lord knows where I would have been if I had decided to allow myself to get lulled into a sense of complacency and carelessness. Nearly a decade later, the business is much stronger than it was. I attribute much of that to the large-scale failure that nearly turned into a full-on collapse of the company. You must know that failure is not always something so obvious. Sometimes failure is one decision away. One door that you open, that leads to it. Sometimes failure can come from outside sources, but, more often than not, it comes from within. Failure is always a choice, but is sometimes disguised.

Which brings me to this: you must understand what failure actually looks like. For instance, I personally do not view someone who came up short as someone who necessarily failed. Athletes who go to the Olympics and compete on behalf of their country would not be looked on as a failure for not bringing home a gold medal. Instead, they are still congratulated and praised for going above and beyond in order to gain the opportunity to compete internationally. You putting in the work, and putting in the time and effort and not getting the exact result that you expected does not mean that you have failed. A long-distance runner who completes their first marathon after months of training is not a failure for not coming in first place. Failure is subjective. Its definition can change based on the original goal, the situation, and the resources that you were given. It is not something that is so black and white. However, the only opinion on what failure is, is your own. People will always say what they will and you cannot please everyone. You will form your own opinions on your actions and whether there was a success or setback as a result. There is a very fine line between failure and success. You, the person in charge, will find yourself toeing the line at times. You will have those moments where it is nose to the grindstone, and you must stay focused. Keep your goals in front of you. I have implored many of my workers to physically write their own personal goals down. There have been many studies by several different groups on the importance of writing out your goals and aspirations.

One study, performed by Dr. Gail Matthews at the Dominican University in California, found that out of the 267 people that she had gathered, the ones who stated that they actually write down their goals on a daily basis were 42% more likely to achieve them. Each morning when you wake up, it may do wonders for you to sit for a second and write down what you want to accomplish for that day. When you first arrive at the office, at the workplace, the classroom, or the job site, you will have a good idea of what you need to accomplish. This will help you stay accountable for your own actions, as well as avoid the possibility of failure by making sure that you are constantly working and growing.

With failure, you can complain about it and move on, or you can learn from it and move on. Either way, you have to move on. But if you decide to complain and not take SOMETHING from it, then you have essentially wasted your time for nothing. Find the silver lining. Find the positive that is hidden behind all of the negatives, and internalize it. A failure is the ending of an opportunity and the beginning of another. As long as you are breathing, you have time to change your story from one of disappointment and despair, into one of glory and victory.

On the previous page, I briefly mentioned Walt Disney's story of losing his job at the news station. But have you ever heard the story of the opening day of Disneyland? Originally, bankers, friends, and even Walt's brother Roy, warned Walt against this venture. They explained to him how such an amusement park had never before existed, and would be a waste of money. Somehow, Walt was able to sell his vision and use his skills as a leader in order to persuade his peers to at least attempt it. To put it mildly, the first day was a complete failure, and probably confirmed what others had said, at least for a little while. Many rides were broken down. The plumbing was never finished, so bathrooms and water fountains were useless. The temperature in Anaheim that day reached one hundred degrees and, as a result–the freshly finished asphalt grew sticky, catching the shoes of many visitors and leaving them stuck in the tar.

These issues, added to the fact that there was two times as many visitors as originally allowed due to counterfeit tickets. This left Walt devastated. He was forced to hold a press conference shortly after to both apologize and attempt to explain the issues which had occurred. Reporters were referring to as "Black Sunday."

While many would have taken this failure and cut their losses, Walt saw opportunity. Walt knew that he had gotten off to a rough start. He understood the fact that his first impression with the public had put a bad taste in their mouth. Walt, however, understood that while first impressions are important, they are not everything. He knew that he could still salvage his dream and turn his story in tone of success. So Walt began to develop a plan to change what had started out as a poor executed beginning. He told the press that he would fix the problems that he had witnessed, and also admitted that it could possibly take a month before things were running smoothly. Walt kept his promises, and quickly corrected the issues that Disneyland had experienced. In just seven weeks after opening day, attendance had soared to over one million visitors. The rest is history. Today, more than 750 million people have visited Disneyland, not including those who have visited Disney World and its resorts.

I tell this story to further help others understand the importance of failure. Life is going to hit you. It is going to knock you down, beat you up, and call you names. If you are not prepared for failure and you do not know how to handle it, success will not come to you. Walt saw what he needed to change, acted on it, and his vision became a reality. Critics had nothing to say, failure had become a distant memory, and his dream was realized. But what does this mean for us, who may be working on a goal that is on a smaller scale than what Walt Disney was striving to achieve? Simple. It is time to stop giving up. There is no person who became successful today by giving up yesterday. Stop giving up on your dream. Stop giving up on your vision. Stop giving up on your team. Stop giving up on yourself.

Only when we can accomplish these tasks will we as leaders become unstoppable. I believe that a person with a purpose is one of the most powerful things that God has ever created. I know that many have heard the saying from various speakers and movies, and it may be overused but it is true: when you want to succeed as much as you want to breathe, you will be successful. When failure and discouragement are unable to deter you from what you have set out to accomplish, then it will be accomplished.

What can we do when failure is inevitable? We can change our tactics, and, if we still find ourselves in the midst of failure, we can find the silver lining, analyze it, and internalize it. Take what you learn (and you need to learn something from it) and use it to change your own paradigm. Use this incident and these feelings of hurt and broaden your horizons with them. Keep an open mind when faced with failure, stay on task, and work through it. You can weather the storm and you can come out of it as a stronger leader than you were when you went in. This is something that we as leaders simply must do. Deal with the failure. Analyze. Internalize. Transform. Repeat process.

"My flesh and my heart may fail, but God is the strength of my heart and my portion forever" –Psalms 73:26

CHAPTER 7

Teaching Yourself How to Teach

"Everybody is a genius. But if you judge a fish on its ability to climb a tree, it will live its whole life believing that it is stupid." – Albert Einstein

Do you remember your favorite teacher back in school? Why were they your favorite? How do you feel they positively impacted you in your life? For me, personally, I would not say that I had a "favorite" teacher per say, yet I do have one that positively impacted me. I was in the third grade, and his name was Mr. Whitehurst.

For some backstory, I was the type of kid back in school who really gave my teachers a run for their money. I talked, I liked to goof off and was a bit of a class clown. Mr. Whitehurst, however, was a no-nonsense type of guy who wanted to teach his lessons and call it a day. I, on the other hand, always seemed to have a different idea on how my day should go.

From the time that I begin schooling until about the end of the eighth grade, teachers could paddle students. Corporal punishment was commonplace in those days; not like now. One day, during a particularly long day in which Mr. Whitehurst was essentially fed up with my antics, grabbed me and paddled me over his desk in front of the entire classroom. He did not have a proper paddle or switch, and used a textbook to do so! My face burned with embarrassment, and I never was a problem child again, at least not in his class!

At the time, I detested Mr. Whitehurst. How could the guy embarrass me like that in front of everyone? I was angry and upset about the situation, but also knew that I had gotten away with a lot more than most. Mr. Whitehurst may have only been trying to get me to sit down and behave and stop interrupting the class. Without doubt, he actually taught me about humility. He put things into perspective, and made me realize at an early age that other people are just as important as you. My interruptions and daily antics would get other students off task and distract them from the lessons that he had worked hard to teach.

There is something about getting paddled by a frustrated teacher in front of all of your peers that really grabs your attention. It shook me and made me think about what I had been doing to Mr. Whitehurst and my fellow classmates.

So, Mr. Whitehurst, if you are alive and well and happen to be reading this, thank you for that!

Mr. Whitehurst, although his methods are different from what I would recommend in the workplace, was the leader of the classroom. He found a way to reach me, and let me know what he was trying to convey. Just as he did, in order to be a successful leader of change, you first must know how to effectively reach your team. Then they will understand what you are trying to convey. Leaders must understand that we will be looked on as the teacher or professor of the workplace. We, therefore, must have an understanding on what grabs the team's attention, and how to better help them internalize knowledge and ideas. It is a common fact amongst educators that people learn in a variety of different ways. By being able to realize the varies techniques that help your team learn, you will be able to get the most out of them in nearly every aspect of the job. There is much debate on the number of different styles of learning, but Dr. Howard Gardner has described seven major styles of intelligence.

The first major style of intelligence is known as visual-spatial. Visual-spatial individuals are those who are quite aware of their surrounding spaces. Often you will find that visual-spatial people enjoy activities, such as jigsaw puzzles or other puzzles, that involve them building and creating things. They will often be benefitted when an educator uses tools like graphs, pictures, drawings and sketches, videos, and models. At the same time you will find visual-spatial types excelling in jobs such as graphic artists, architects, and other art-based jobs.

The second major style of intelligence is what Dr. Gardner refers to as bodily-kinesthetic. This type of person finds interest in communicating through use of their own body. What Dr. Gardner means by that is that bodily-kinesthetic individuals enjoy movement, they take pleasure out of making things with their hands. They will often rely on hands-on learning activities to further their understanding of lessons. They take pleasure from using their hands and physical activity. Common jobs for this style would be dancers, actors, physical therapists, mechanics, and carpenters.

The third major style of intelligence would be musical. Musical is exactly how it sounds, music! Musical types respond positively to rhythm and sound. They love music itself, but also seem to respond to various sounds within their environment. Some musical types enjoy playing music as they work or when they study, as it helps them to better focus. Musical-type people enjoy the use of musical instruments or watching videos that incorporate music within their jobs. Common jobs would be musicians, or various other occupations within the music industry.

The fourth major style of intelligence is known as interpersonal. Interpersonal people enjoy interacting and understanding other people around them. These types of individuals learn directly through interaction, and will often have a wide variety of friends from various walks of life. Interpersonal people find that they learn best in group activities and dialogues. They consider themselves to be extroverted, and enjoy conversing with one another. They can also learn directly through time and conversation with the instructor. An interpersonal individual is a people person, plain and simple. Nurses, psychologists, and various types of managers will often consider themselves to be an interpersonal-type person.

The fifth major style of intelligence discussed by Dr. Gardner is known as intra-personal. Intra-personal people are nearly the exact opposite of interpersonal people. People who are intra-personal tend to focus less on understanding others around them and more on trying to understand themselves. They pay attention to their own goals and morals, and are more introverted than extroverted. Whereas an interpersonal individual would be the outgoing, social butterfly. The intra-personal person tends to be shy. They can be taught through their own independent studying, and will often take pleasure in activities such as reading and writing. Intra-personal types are the most independent of all seven major styles of intelligence. Common occupations would be entrepreneurs, theologians, and philosophers.

The sixth major style of intelligence is called Linguistic. Linguistic individuals enjoy using words to help convey whatever it is that they are trying to convey. They realize the power and effect that words can have on others. Linguistic-type individuals often have strong auditory skills and think about the connotations that specific words have. Linguistic types, like the intra-personal types, enjoy reading and writing. While intra-personal tend to be more serious, linguistics will often write poetry or stories in addition to more serious subjects. Some linguistic types will learn through usage of various games, using computers, or listening to lectures from instructors. Common occupations amongst linguistic types would be translators, writers, speech and language therapists, and journalists.

The seventh and final major style of intelligence that Dr. Gardner recognizes is called logical-mathematical. Those who fall into the style known as logical-mathematical utilize reasoning and calculations. They tend to think abstractly, and notice various patterns throughout life. They will learn by forming relationships in their head with other previous ideas. While details can prove to be difficult for them, they will first internalize concepts before discussing details of plans and ideas. Common jobs for those who are logical-mathematical types would be scientists, auditors, accountants, computer analysts, and mathematicians.

What does this mean for your team? Well, it can mean quite a bit. Maybe some of you reading about these seven styles of intelligence were thinking about a team member you have. Often, we as leaders make mistakes. One of the most common mistakes that I have witnessed, and been a part of personally, is the fact that many great workers with strong passions and dreams are stuck in a position or business that does not challenge them on a daily basis. We discussed this in chapter 3 when discussing how we fit the pieces together, and again in chapter 5 when I told about my lack of passion for my blue-collar job in the electrical union. You have to recognize when a good worker is stuck in something that he or she is not passionate about. You must be able to fit them into a role in which they will be successful for you and for themselves.

But these seven styles of intelligence are not just for you to utilize amongst your own team. You are a part of the team, and will need to apply this knowledge to yourself as well. For those reading, maybe you recognized yourself amongst the seven major groups. Maybe you did not, and fall into one of the hundreds of other subcategories. Chances are, you recognized bits and pieces of yourself in several different major categories. This is extremely common, and the next part is going to be shocking and confusing to some readers:

Most people fall into multiple categories.

This can obviously make your job as a leader and as a teacher extremely difficult. How can we be expected to efficiently teach our team if they can be hundreds, if not THOUSANDS of different combinations of intelligence styles? We must utilize a wide variety of techniques and tactics in order to be sure that we have reached and captivated everyone in the room.

For example, some of your team may benefit greatly from a lecture in which they take down notes and study them in their leisure. Others may be bored and cannot help but to tune you out, regardless of your level of excitement during the lecture. Others may prefer group based activities within their peer group, while some will feel anxious and uncomfortable during these activities. You must use as many different learning activities as you can. Research the various things that teachers come up with in their classrooms. You are a professional at leading others. You may not necessarily be the best at educating. In order to educate, you must first be educated on how to do so.

We, as leaders, may need to do our own homework in order to understand how best to reach the masses. By listening to what your team has to say about the activities, you will be able to understand what style of intelligence they may fall into. This is going to take some understanding and a lot of attention to detail. You must channel your interpersonal style, even if that is not your forte! You must pay attention to the tasks they do in their daily lives in order to better determine what they prefer and how they internalize ideas. Do they seem to talk to others around them or do they keep to themselves? Will they write down notes descriptively that they then study, or do they seem to stare and ask questions during lectures instead of write anything down. These are questions that you will need to be able to answer when looking at the people in your team that you are accountable for. By creating a positive environment where everyone is assisted in understanding processes, protocols, ideas, and goals, those around you will have a better understanding of what is expected of them, as well as how they are able to reach the goals set out for them. Sometimes, leaders can interpret a misunderstanding or miscommunication as insubordination or otherwise disobedience.

By ensuring that you have explained and taught the processes in multiple ways, and have expressed it clearly to every member of the group, you will lessen these misunderstandings and frustrations. When every member of the team is striving towards the same goal, everyone must be on the same page. I like to compare this idea to the concept of a rowing team. If the members of the left side of the row boat are rowing when the members of the right side are not ready, the boat will only spin in circles. You must have everyone set to the same pace, working together, and working smarter rather than harder.

As the leader of the boat, you are in charge of making the decision on when to do what, and on coordinating and influencing the cooperation of others on the team. Together, you can race to the finish and come out on top. As leaders, we must find better ways to do that, and, in my opinion, it starts with communicating on the same level as every member of your team. Speak to their strengths rather than weaknesses. Interpret and understand their styles of learning and take them into account.

Another part of this technique that may prove to be difficult is the fact that many people do not know which style of intelligence that they mostly rely on. Remember how I said that there are hundreds of subcategories? Perhaps some of you reading this did not find themselves lumped into any one specific category. Maybe you yourself have no idea what it is that helps you to understand and internalize bits of information. This is also common. Chances are, your team will not be able to outright tell you what works for them specifically. It will be up for you to find out and then use to your advantage. They will either take something from your lecture or game or explanation, or they will not.

When they do not seem to grasp the concept that you are trying to convey, you will need to change your tactic to suit their needs. Lecture did not work? Maybe it is time to try out a group activity. This still has not work? Perhaps you should use graphs and statistics to further your point. Send out an email that others can read and reread while taking notes on it. Find a video that maybe furthers your idea. Some will grasp the concepts after the first discussion, others may take a bit longer. Some will benefit from the group activity and understand, while others may still need some other form of educating in order for them to fully get it. This takes patience. All great teachers have patience for their students. It takes diligence and determination on your part, as great teachers will not quit on their students. Your team will be very similar to the students in a classroom, in the sense that they look to you, the educator, for guidance and assistance in their day-to-day lives and tasks.

You must also take care to convey your messages and provide your team with knowledge while also not coming across as feeling superior or otherwise better than them. I like to relate this concept to Luke 6:40, which states:

"The student is not above their teacher, but everyone who is fully trained will be like their teacher."

As leaders, our biggest joy will be seeing our team rise to the point where they essentially lead themselves regardless of whether we are present or not. Leaders teach and are essentially trying to instill the positive qualities within themselves into the members of their team. Therefore, while we do make the final decision on many different aspects in our job, we must approach our team as an equal who only wants what is best for the team and the company. By being approachable and open with your team, you will gain the opportunity for your team to speak their minds on the various techniques that you are utilizing in order to better train and educate them. This is a scenario in which you will adamantly require their communication and feelings on the situation. This will be the only way in which you know for a fact that a team member has understood a concept that you have conveyed. You, as a leader and an educator, will also need to take the manner in which you reinforce or counter behaviors. How do you handle the triumphs and tribulations of a team member on a small scale? Do you celebrate or ignore their successes? Do you explain or argue with their objections or setbacks? This will bring us to our next topic within this specific chapter.

An important concept to understand would be called operant conditioning. Operant conditioning was a concept that was developed by American psychologist B.F. Skinner. Operant conditioning is defined as roughly and immediately changing of behavior by the use of reinforcement, which is given after the desired or undesired behavior. In short, this refers to the idea of punishment and reward, which will change the behavior of individuals. These processes or ideas of reward and punishment are referred to by B.F. Skinner as positive and negative reinforcement. We will have to understand what positive and negative reinforcement looks like within the workplace, as well as when to use positive or negative reinforcement. There will be pros and cons to both positive and negative reinforcement, and both tactics will affect team members differently. By understanding your team on an individual level, you will be able to better determine how each person will respond to the two different types of reinforcement.

Positive reinforcement would be the reward for a specific behavior. Examples would be getting an allowance as a child for doing all of your chores, or receiving praise for getting good grades in school. For the workplace, bonuses and raises in exchange for individuals hitting their goals and going above and beyond that which is expected of them. You see, even as adults, many people take pleasure in their hard work being noticed by their leaders. By telling someone how great a job that they did, or simply mentioning that you are impressed, it will do wonders for their self-esteem as well as their work ethic. This is a concept that I have struggled with in the past. It's something that I feel some other leaders in their respective areas of expertise can struggle with as well. Sometimes it is easy to overlook a success if it is minor or if you have other tasks going on.

While you may not think twice about it, your team can take it as you snubbing them or deeming their success as something minute and insignificant. Make sure that they know that they are appreciated and positively reinforce the behavior that you want to see repeated throughout their workday. Little things such as taking the team out for lunch because they hit an all-time high with their numbers, or giving out gift cards to those who have done exceptional work for that week can go a long way for your team. For this, you do not even necessarily have to make any monetary contribution more often than not, as a simple "thank you" is priceless to you and something that is worth more than money to your team. There is no measure to how important it is to feel appreciated and needed by your leaders. Acknowledge their successes, let them know that their successes are your successes. The growth of the individuals on your team will, in turn, help to grow the team and company as a whole.

If positive reinforcement would be the reward for a specific behavior, then negative reinforcement would be the punishment for a specific behavior. Examples would be talking with and reprimanding a team member for having a poor attitude or being rude towards other members, or, on a larger scale, writing up an employee for various incidents of insubordination.

The fact is, no one likes negative reinforcement. I do not take joy out of getting onto my team, nor does my team take joy out of me reprimanding them. Negative reinforcement can be awkward and uncomfortable and, depending on the situation, can lead to a hostile environment. As a leader, you do not want this. Negative reinforcement, however, is necessary. For some, it is the only way that they will be able to internalize what you are trying to explain, while others will close up and become ineffective in their jobs when faced with negative reinforcement. But negative reinforcement does not have to be outright confrontational. A simple comment such as "we as a team should be careful and take care to not do this" is an example of negative reinforcement on a small scale that will get your point across without being offensive or rude to those around you. For some, negative reinforcement should be handled with care and understanding, whereas others need to be specifically told what they are doing that is wrong or not allowed before they know that they must change their behavior and ways of thinking.

B.F. Skinner tested his theories and ideas of operant conditioning back in the 1930s and 1940s through use of what is now commonly referred to as a Skinner box. This box had a metal grid running along the bottom, which had electrical wire attached to it. A small lab rat would be placed in the box, and, over a period of time, the rat was taught how to press buttons and pull a lever that was inside the box. When the rat would pull the lever, the rat was rewarded with a piece of food that would be dispensed into the box.

As a result, the rat would often pull the lever in order to receive the snack. The rat understood that when he would pull the lever, food would appear. This is the example of positive reinforcement. The negative reinforcement, although a bit cruel by today's standards, would show the influence that negative reinforcement had on the decisions and behaviors of others. When the rat would click certain buttons, the metal grid would deliver a quick shock to the rat. After a few times, the rat would no longer press those buttons and be fearful when Skinner attempted to get the rat to press them. The rat understood that every time the button was pressed, he would feel an unpleasant shock. For some rats, it took a bit of time to understand the positive and negative reinforcements, while for others it came much quicker. With this psychology experiment, Skinner helped to explain the ideas of positive and negative reinforcement, as well as the importance of having both within a specific environment.

We must take care to be balanced in using both types of reinforcements among our team. We have to set boundaries as well, as celebrate successes in our lives and the individuals of our team. This is something that many leaders, including myself, will have to consciously think about and be aware. It is not something that always comes natural to me, and something that I am better at now than I was ten years ago. I hope to be even better at ten years from now.

As a leader and a teacher, we are always learning about those who are around us. You must train yourself, and teach yourself how to teach in order to lead others. To teach others, you must first be taught. To lead others, you must have been led. Just as other people learn differently and have different styles of intelligence, they will also respond in different manners to positive and negative reinforcement. There are some days in which you will have to play the counselor, the mediator, the leader, the drill sergeant (although on a smaller scale!) and the listener, but every single day that you are a leader, you will also be looked upon as a teacher. The two titles are almost synonymous.

For as long as you lead, you will teach. For as long as you teach, you will be expected to lead. Therefore, it is important as a leader of any business in any industry to also understand the psychology and importance behind teaching others. There is a method to the madness when it comes to teaching. Teaching can be hectic and can take up a lot of your day. If you are willing to put in the time and put forth the effort, you will be able to accomplish the task.

Just as Jesus himself was a great teacher and understood the importance of teaching lessons to his students and disciples, we as leaders on a much smaller scale, should follow in his footsteps and teach those around us to be the absolute best that they can possibly be. This will stretch you as a person and leader, and them as a worker and student. You see, teaching asks something of you and of the student both. It requires hard work on both ends, as well as the ability to handle stress and be persistent. Many of your team may not get what you are trying to express the first time (remember, not everyone learns in the same manner) and as a result, you will have to go over certain tactics, policies, and ideas more than once. It can be frustrating, but understand that it is OKAY. This is often a part of the process for us leaders and teachers.

Being an effective teacher is more than just standing in front of a podium and talking until your time is up or you run out of things to say. Being a teacher takes some skill, some know-how. For some leaders this may come easy, while for others it may prove to be a stretch. You may not be a people person, you may feel awkward while teaching your team. You may even not fully understand how to go about this. This is where you will have to study yourself. You, and you alone, will be the only person who can effectively teach you how to teach. By looking up various techniques and tactics that teachers use, as well as getting to know your team specifically, you will be able to reach them. By studying the individuals around you, you will get a better sense of how they learn, what they respond to, and how to approach them and get the best results out of it.

"All scripture is breathed out by God and profitable for teaching, for reproof, for correction, and for training in righteousness" – 2 Timothy 3:16

CHAPTER 8

Leading Efficiently and Effectively

"Efficiency is doing things right. Effectiveness is doing the right things." – Peter F. Drucker

There have been times in my 20+ years as an entrepreneur and leader that I have been effective, but not efficient. By that same token, there have been times where I was so worried about being efficient that I did not stop to wonder whether or not I was being effective. Efficiency will save you time and money, while effectiveness will save you some frustration. It will help you finish whatever task or goal that you are trying to accomplish. I have compiled a total of ten tips that I feel have helped me personally to become more effective as well as more efficient in my day-to-day life.

The first tip that I have in order to become more efficient and effective as a leader would be that being in charge is not a popularity contest. Make your decisions without any concern for whether people like you or agree with you. By this, I do not mean to be dictatorial leader by any means. In previous chapters, I have discussed how important it can be for your team to enjoy your company and agree with you. This is true, to an extent.

As humans, it is natural to feel empathy and understand another person's point of view. I understand that, and believe that it is important at times to take the voices of others in the team and consider their ideas. However, you are the leader and your decision is the final say. It should truly be YOUR decision and not that of someone else. Ultimately, you are the leader for a reason, and you are completely responsible for your company's successes as well as their failures.

While others liking you will make your job easier in some situations, only you will make the final decision. You sign the check. You make the rules. You make the decision to change a policy or scheduling or who is in charge of what. You need to set aside your personal relationships and feelings about those who are around you in order to make the hard decisions that are best for the company. I know that this is a difficult task.

We like to please others. I consider myself to be a people pleaser. It can be important in some situations for others to like us. In fact, you need to have a bit of charisma as a leader in order for others to follow you. I like to say that a leader without followers is just a person taking a walk. But anyone who has been, is currently, or ever will be a leader knows for a fact that leadership is not easy. If you want to be an effective leader, sometimes you will be required to make tough choices. Often these choices will not be popular amongst the team, but they will be necessary.

In some cases, the team will actually prefer it, believe it or not. For instance, in times of extreme crisis and struggles, when the team around you seems to be panicking or unsure as to what they should do, the team will look to you and need you to be a decisive leader who has no qualms about taking charge and forming the game plan on your own. If you have the absolute desire for your team and for the individuals that you are leading to be better and for the company to be better, than your decisions should eventually turn out to be okay.

The second tip that I have for a leader to become more efficient and effective would be when making changes to the status quo. Explain your reasons and emphasize that the results will prove beneficial for your organization as a whole. When you are changing or deviating from the norm that everyone else is used to, explain your reasoning and ideas behind the change. The people who want to achieve the same goals as you will get on board. I firmly believe that effective leaders will shake and then shatter the status quo. I do not want or like things to be stagnant. Not in my personal life or in my business. You must be doing something, and at times I feel as if I would rather be moving backwards than staying in the same place as I was yesterday. Do SOMETHING! Do not simply stay there and do nothing and expect results. Be sure when explaining your reasons for changing the status quo that you emphasize the fact that you are changing the normal policies or operations in order to benefit the company and those who are involved with it. If you are going to make changes of any kind, explain the reasons for why you have decided to make these changes. Talk to your team about the benefits of these changes and why you have decided to deviate from what you had previously put in place. If others in the team are not on board, then they will most likely see themselves off board, and that is okay too. You as a leader will need to do what is best for your team. Again, it is your decision, not anyone else's.

The third tip is something that is common amongst effective and efficient leaders. If you are looking to build a successful organization, you will require two things: a clear plan for the future, and the courage to stick to that plan. For those who absolutely love football (Go Bucs!), have you ever noticed how during the halftime interviews, the really good coaches do not just write their team off as a terrible team who needs to completely change the game plan? The solid and successful coaches will state that they need to execute the game plan and play the game the way that they discussed and practiced on in the weeks leading up to the game. The same goes for a successful organization. You and I both must have a clear plan for what we need to do, and then we in turn must have the courage and determination to stick to the game plan that we had come up with previously. When the going gets tough and the stress begins to get to you, you cannot just throw what you had out of the window. Take the good with the bad, and execute your strategy as best as you can. If you are going to go somewhere significant, then you are going to have some hurdles and some roadblocks. It is not going to be peachy and covered with rainbows. The road is going to be difficult at times. Stick with your plan.

The fourth tip I would like to state here is that the most important building block of team success is attitude. If your organization has an attitude problem, address that situation first. Attitude, as Zig Ziglar says, will determine your altitude. I believe that many talented and intelligent people do not reach their full potential in life simply because their attitude prohibited them from doing that. Your attitude will determine your altitude... and your income! There are times within my company where I essentially had to clean house. I had to let people go who were around me and my team. I felt were they were talented, but their attitude would not allow them to rise above the average and become successful. For your large dreams and visions, an attitude that is anything less than completely on board will simply not suffice. Get on board, get off, or get run over! Your attitude problem, be it with you or your team, has to be addressed. It will poison those around it if it goes unassisted.

The fifth tip would be that team unity should exist both on the field and off. Create avenues for your people to get to know one another outside of strictly business environments. Have a company picnic, invite your team over to your house for a get-together. Take your team for lunch on occasion. Challenge the members of your leadership to come up with ways to get the rest of your crew involved and excited. Understand that everyone has interests that do not involve the office. Go paintballing or bowling, something fun that interests and de-stresses the rest of your group. Some things that I have done in the past with members of my team are golfing or boating. It is something peaceful, relaxing, and fun that everyone can enjoy as a team. It creates bonds and unity amongst your employees which can greatly benefit your company as a whole. The best way to get your leadership team to set up activities like this is to exemplify that yourself. Team unity needs to exist in more areas than just at the business.

My sixth tip for becoming more efficient and effective as a leader would be that it may be impossible to treat everyone in the same way, but it is possible to treat everyone fairly. Make fairness your major ambition. Note that I did not say simply giving out handouts to those who have not yet earned it, nor am I professing a belief in a socialist frame of mind. Sometimes things will not be the same for every single person, but you should make it fair so that everyone who is a part of the business has the chance for growth in his or her respected areas of expertise.

My seventh tip would be that superstars within the business should not receive special treatment. This is a sure ingredient for a breakdown in team cohesion. I know that this is a difficult idea to implement for those like myself who are performance driven leaders. I am one of the most performance driven leaders and people that I personally know. But doing this is a surefire ingredient for team breakdown. It can be extremely discouraging for other members of the team to witness this. It is okay to spend time with your superstars or to recognize who your superstars are. But superstars still should not receive special or otherwise preferential treatment for doing their jobs.

The eighth tip that I have in order to be effective and efficient leaders would be to follow your instincts. There is no textbook for leadership success. Sometimes you will uncover unortho-dox methods that may not work for others, but work for you. There is no set rules or textbook to assist you with the plethora of challenges and setbacks that you will face as a leader. As the saying goes, if it isn't broke, don't fix it! If what you are doing is working and making you and your team successful, keep on doing it! Trust in your own judgement and trust in your own instincts.

The ninth tip that I am giving is that when things do go wrong, recognize that small, incremental changes may be all that is needed to right the ship. Notice that I say WHEN things go wrong and not IF, as being a leader who is heading in the right, you will face adversity at some point in your career. But small changes may make all the difference. You do not necessarily need to completely change and revamp the organization, nor to you need to completely start over in most cases. Nine times out of ten, you will simply need to add just a few small tweaks in order to be successful. Stay on course and follow the path. Take a small shift to the left, a tiny turn to the right. Be like a captain of a sailboat. Make little adjustments, avoid the rocky areas, brace yourself for impacts against the waves, and come out on top. Sometimes you will need to shift to a lower gear and slow down, while others you will need to shift to a higher gear and speed up. Utilize tiny changes in order to right the ship.

The tenth and final tip that I would like to state in this chapter is that as the leader, you set the tone. You have to want to win and be successful more than anyone else in the organization. No one else should want it more than you. If you set a winning tone, it will penetrate and become infectious among every sin-gle person on your team. If your organization fails, it is your fault as a leader. If my organization fails, it is my fault as a leader. With that in consideration, you must set the tone in your organization. Do not be too bashful or uncertain to be the voice who says that we will be victorious and that we can do it. You must want the success as badly as you want to breathe. It is not up to anyone else; you will not have any help in that aspect of your job as a leader. By the same token, you should not want the success of any individual in your organization more than they want it for themselves. When you are in a room full of individuals who want to be successful, you as a team can accomplish anything that you set your minds too.

These ten tips were not necessarily something that I sat down and came up with randomly. Instead, these ten tips were things that I learned through trial and error, success and failure, and victory and defeat. I learned these ten tips on being an efficient and effective leader by being a leader and discovering what worked for me and what most certainly did not. I said previously that should I write a book on failure, it would contain thousands of chapters. It is these failures that have taught me such lessons as those tips listed above.

I believe that being efficient and effective is more than just working faster and getting your point across. I believe that efficiency is when someone finds a way to work smarter and not harder. Efficiency is nothing more than intelligent laziness. Bill Gates has said that he will always choose a lazy person to complete a difficult task, because the lazy individual will find an easier way to accomplish the task. What he meant by this, is that in terms of efficiency, it is completely okay and preferred to find a way to get more work done in less amount of time. Efficiency can come from implementing newer technology, such as when we discussed Henry Ford's implementing of the automobile assembly line system, or, from simply adding more people to your team who are intelligent and qualified to perform the tasks that you need done on a daily basis.

More often than not, efficiency comes on a small scale. It starts directly with the individuals on your team. It can start with one member finding out a way to accomplish their daily tasks without cutting out anything important. Perhaps they are a salesman who finds out a good phrase to use when speaking with a client, or maybe they are a worker in a warehouse, who learns of a way to speed up their tasks without as much strain on their body. In any industry, efficiency can be improved. I believe in the power and unpredictability of people. It is crazy to think that you can give ten different people the same task, and all ten could come up with different ways to accomplish it. Rather than cut corners or do something half-heartedly, the hard-working individuals will find a way to complete the task entirely, only with less time and effort involved. As long as they are coming to the same conclusion when all is said and done, I am completely okay with them finding other ways to make their daily tasks easier and quicker. The time that your team saves by being more efficient will provide them with the opportunity to work on other projects, brainstorm for ideas to help the organization, and train and perfect their craft. As a leader and business owner, efficiency can be your best friend. But it takes innovation. It takes having an intelligent grouping of people around you. It takes open-mindedness and brain-storming meetings and hard work to figure it out.

I give these ten tips in order to provide other leaders like my-self with tools that I was once provided with. These tips, al-though they can be difficult to accomplish and implement at times, are necessary in order to boost your effectiveness and efficiency as a leader, be it on a small scale or a large scale. If you feel as if you are already implementing these, great! Keep at it. Keep working diligently. The effectiveness and efficiency will come. If you have not been using these tips, and you feel as if you could greatly improve your effectiveness and effi-ciency, I implore you to try them out. Take the tips to heart, keep them in the back of your mind at all times, and utilize them when you see the opportunity to do so. Issues may start with leadership and management, but they can also be stopped with leadership and management.

Yet another trait that I feel we as leaders will need to possess would be what I refer to as tough-skin. If you do not have this by now as a leader, you will need to develop this quickly. We have discussed in the tips that as leaders of change, we will often have to make decisions that are not easy.

Some decisions will not be popular, and you may disagree with other members of the team at times. This can lead to complications and frustration on both your end as well as your team. You will have to figure out a way to keep a cool head and handle stress and frustration. If I had not been able to learn how to do this, I would never have gotten my vision out to the world and you would not be holding this book right now. It isn't easy. It isn't fun. It is not for the faint of heart or the weak–minded. It is tough. You will deal with adversity and you will be expected to deal with it. As a leader, you can sit and cry during times of stress and hardship, or you can get up, dust yourself off, and handle what needs to be handled. This is going to take thick skin. If every little thing seems to set you off in your organization, you are going to have a very difficult time being an effective and efficient leader.

Leadership (and therefore teaching) is where everything that either succeeds or fails hinges. Having a strong or weak leadership will directly correlate to the success or failure of your organization. Being able to effectively lead your team is the most important part. We do not have lectures for our own amusement. We are not there to feed our ego (or should not be, at least) nor are we merely there to take a paycheck and sit back and relax. A leader leads, and leads with enthusiasm. You must take note of whether you are effectively making waves in your business. Once you are absolutely certain that you can be effective, then you will be able to focus on efficiency. You see, just as an infant will crawl before they can walk, they will walk before they can run. Learn how to be effective, and learn how to get your team involved first, and then you will have the opportunity to learn how to do your job faster. Throughout my time not only at my own company, but at various businesses and churches in which I have been a part of, I have learned one major thing about people: they want to be led. People respond to strong and effective leadership. They respect it, understand the importance of it, and, if it applies to them, they will follow it. People feel safe in knowing that even if a catastrophe or unforeseeable issue arises, that they will have a strong and flexible leader who is able to effectively lead them through the storm and on to better days. Whether it is a church congregation who responds positively to their enthusiastic and knowledgeable pastor, or a small company in which the team has their trust in their leaders and management, people want to be led. It is up to the leader to keep them captivated and continue to find ways to lead them effectively. You are the captain of the ship. You will either lead them to where the goal destination is, or you will wind up like the captain of the Titanic! Choices, processes, and proper use of the tools that God has given you will determine your fate, as well as the fate of the organization as a whole.

Choices and processes will also determine whether you are effective and efficient at hitting your goals. Before you can be effective in reaching your goals, you must first set them for you and your team. A goal is defined as the object of a person's ambition or effort, or the aim of their desired result. Your ambition as a leader is your desire, what you want, what you are passionate about. A goal is an object that is birthed from your ambition and your passionate. In order to be an effective leader you must have ambition and be passionate about being a leader in the first place! It must excite you. You cannot successfully accomplish very many things in life while doing them halfheartedly, and this is especially true for leadership. A leader has be to all the way involved. You must make a conscious decision to be an effective leader and find ways to make your job as well as the job of your team members more efficient. If leading is your true passion, then your own goals need to reflect that. If an opportunity for a leadership role presents itself, or perhaps a time for you to be a more effective leader arises, you need to set goals for such occasions and you need to have the passion and ambition that is required in order for you to achieve these goals.

Being efficient is sprinting instead of simply jogging. It is spending the time and effort to be innovative and making your life easier instead of simply working harder than is necessary. Good workers can accomplish their entire day's tasks in eight hours. Great workers find ways to accomplish their entire day's tasks in less time so they can take a breather. Outstanding workers find ways to accomplish their entire day's tasks so they can spend more time working on other projects or tasks within the company. The only way you can expect your team to understand and mirror that type of behavior is through being effective and efficient in your own work. As a leader, if you can implement this yourself and show your team the possibilities and benefits of being more efficient, they will begin to follow suit.

Common ways to boost your level of efficiency on a personal level would be to track and set a limit for yourself on how much time is actually spent on small and unnecessary tasks. By looking at the specific time it takes you, you will see where you can save a few minutes in certain daily tasks. Be sure to set yourself some deadlines that you feel are far enough out to remain effective but short enough to where you will need to be diligent.

Another idea for efficiency would be to be wary of the length of time that your breaks are. While it can be very beneficial to get up, walk around, get a cup of coffee, or catch some fresh air in front of your office building, be aware of exactly how much time per day that you spend not actively working on your goals. If it gets to be a good portion of your day, it will be something that you as a leader will have to change if you are striving to be more effective and efficient. Some of us, as leaders, will have to work at getting better with our time management skills. For some they can do this easily, while others may find that this is where their weakness lies. Make sure to pay attention to how you manage your time, and whether or not it seems to work for you.

Similarly, to be more efficient is to start early. Almost every morning, I grab a cup of espresso from Starbucks on the way to the office. By the time I have arrived, I am awake, alert, I have my cup of coffee so I do not waste time grabbing any. When I arrive at work, I am here to work. From the moment that I park my car until the moment I head out of the office. When you are at work, be at work! As a leader, you will find yourself fighting against the clock on some days in order to hit your goals and help your team hit theirs. By making sure that you come to work prepared and ready to go, you will be able to make the best out of the time that you have been given.

You may already be a good leader. You may even be a great leader. But there is always room for improvement. You never stop learning how to be a better leader, and one of your goals every day should be to be a more effective and efficient leader today than you were yesterday. Lead your team by creating an effective environment in which they will be able to learn alongside you the ways in which you all, as a unit, will be able to come up with new ways to boost the efficiency and effectiveness of your work. Lead efficiently and effectively. Do not jog when you have learned how to sprint!

"Whatever you do, give it your very best, as if you were working for the master and not for human beings." – Colossians 3:23

CHAPTER 9

Rise and Shine

"Work hard, stay positive, and get up early. It's the best part of the day." – George Allen Sr.

It was early in the morning, still dark outside. I was wide awake, thinking about my day and ideas began to fill my head. I reached out, grabbed my phone, and started to set little reminders for myself. I began to send out emails of the ideas that had come to me, in order to jot them down and share them while they were fresh in my mind. I was cautious to do this quickly, so as not to spare even the most trivial of details. At this point, I decided to send my father a text about something that I was supposed to help him with that day. I expected that he would receive the text later on in the morning and respond once he was up. To my surprise, I heard the distinct *"ping"* from my iPhone indicating that I had received a notification. It was from my dad and he had responded to my text. Before I knew it, we were having a conversation through text message about the matter in which he needed my help. The lesson suddenly clicked for me: top performers are engaged in their business and they are striving for success from the minute their feet hit the ground every morning.

I remember my father saying: "an early riser like me, huh?' to which I replied with, "you know it!" I believe that it is in the early waking hours that our minds are the sharpest. It is at the beginning of the day that we have the privilege, opportunity, and the responsibility of setting the foundation of which the remainder of our day will be built. We have yet to experience any defeat or stress, nor have we had the chance to face the many obstacles that the day may have in store for us. In the early morning, anything for that day is still possible and our motivation and passion can be endless. Our attitudes should be that of a positive and optimistic one.

The old adage, "rise and shine" comes to mind. This phrase originated back in the 1800s as a military order that meant to act lively and behave well. It is not enough to simply rise; we must shine as well! It may be dark outside and you may have had a rough day. Half of the world is probably curled up, asleep in their beds, but you are awake and you are ready to shine.

This is what separates the strong from the weak. The champions from the challengers. The lions from the lambs. The leaders from the managers. If we want to win, we must be a step ahead of our competition, and this starts with you waking up in the morning. One of my favorite quotes is by an unknown author, and it reads:

"Every morning in Africa, a gazelle wakes up It knows that it must run faster than the fastest lion or it will be killed. Every morning, a lion wakes up as well. The lion knows that it must outrun the slowest gazelle or else it will starve. It does not matter whether you are a gazelle or a lion...when the sun comes up, you better be running."

Now I don't know about you, but personally? I would hate to be beaten in any contest by someone else because they had arrived before I did. If we are both there, and it is a fair contest, and I lose, then so be it. But if the contest is over before I had even started to compete, then it is my fault entirely for missing the occasion. I refuse to lose OR to win by default. I want some competition. I want the opportunity for myself to fail, but I also want the opportunity for myself to succeed. By missing the chance and letting someone else take a shot, you are losing by default.

We have all heard it said before: "I am not a morning person." Or: "I hate having to wake up early." The fact is that you don't HAVE to wake up early, but rather you GET to wake up early. View your mornings as an early opportunity to start before your competitors. You have a free head start, use it to your advantage. There are no fair fights. This is competition and while your competitor sleeps, you are training. You go the extra distance.

There is an old Japanese proverb that says:

"Cry in the dojo, and you will smile on the battlefield."

Do the extra little bit while you can; that way you will have an easier workload later on during crunch time. If we want to become a "top performer," then we can help ourselves by getting an early jump on our work in the mornings. In the case of being a top performer who is ready and able as soon as they wake up, you need to learn to become a morning person. Because the early bird truly does get the worm and the worms are precious. When you are second, you will have to settle for the scraps. Scraps are for losers. Lions do not get scraps. The scraps are reserved for vultures and other weaker, less dominant species. Second-place winner is also the first-place loser. Sure, you can get a few scrap worms, and some have probably even lived out their entire career by this way of thinking, but this is not promised. Things may come to those that wait, but only things that have been left by those who were out hustling. Remember that success is not an accident, but rather a state of mind. If we have not yet reached a level that we have originally hoped to reach, then we have to consciously make the changes necessary to do what is required to reach it.

Do not just take my words for the importance of mornings. Do some research on it. Some people who identify themselves as "morning people" would be Mary Barra, the CEO of General Motors. Mary has been known to show up to the office around six in the morning, and has done this long before she was the CEO. Her predecessor, Daniel Akerson, also has made comments about waking up early. Ursula Burns, CEO of Xerox, gets up at five every single morning to start her day, which also consists of personal training at six before she goes into work. The president of Starbucks, Michelle Gass, sips her first cup of coffee around four in the morning when she gets up to go on her daily run. Benjamin Franklin was notorious for planning out his day and sticking to a firm routine. He would contemplate what it was that he would be working on in the mornings while he ate his breakfast. Before his day had even really started, he had a game plan and knew what he needed to focus on.

These immensely successful individuals got up early and some of them continue to get up early each and every day. They know that success is only a place and that it can change very quickly, so they continue to put in the work. These people would much rather have a game plan before they step foot into the office, rather than spending the first hour or so of their work day sitting and planning. Use every minute of your time to your advantage. Time is the most precious tool that you will have as a leader, and you must take care not to waste any of it, as you will never be able to get it back. Time can be your strongest tool, or your worst enemy, depending on how you use it and how you view it. Get up early. Get your coffee. Eat your breakfast. Read the newspaper, read your Bible like I do, and get ready for your daily tasks and obstacles.

There have also been studies that indicate that there may be a direct correlation between morning people and a reported increase in happiness. Renee Bliss, a graduate at the University of Tornoto, found that both younger as well as older people who get up earlier in the morning report experiencing more positive emotions than those who did not often wake up early. In a 2008 study of students at a university in Texas, the students who identified as morning people tended to have GPA's at nearly an entire point higher than their counterparts who would sleep in more often.

Many who normally wake up early have said that they normally do not feel groggy and are fully aware much quicker than others. Some studies have indicated that these people report much lower stress levels, and as such, seem to be nicer, more outgoing, and suffer from depression at a much lower rate than others. Overall, the benefits from getting up earlier greatly outweigh the little to no benefits of sleeping in until later on. I think that you should take your love of sleep and compare it with how badly that you want to be successful. Sit down and write out a list of pros and cons to each. I can almost guarantee you that you will find the list of pros for getting up and getting motivated to be much longer than the pros for staying in bed. Yes, staying in bed will feel good now, but it surely will not later. Waking up early can be difficult at first, but once you make it a habit then it becomes a great start to the day.

Understand that every single day that you wake up, and you are healthy and ready, is a new day. From the moment that you opened your eyes and took your head off of your pillow, you are capable of accomplishing anything. That day is yours; do with it what you will. You can take it and make it into a day that is productive and useful, or you can allow it to be wasted. The choice is completely yours. Time is one of the few resources in life that is unrenewable. We will never gain it back, you cannot earn it back, and you have no idea just how much of it that you have at any one point. Time is valuable. Time should not be wasted on doing things that will not directly contribute to your success as a leader.

For me, personally, my body will not allow me to sleep past six in the morning during the week. Some days I find myself up around three or four in the morning, checking my emails and text messages from the night before, sending devotionals to my family and friends, or thinking about what needs to be accomplished for my team and myself today. My normal morning routine is to read my Bible and use it as my motivation for the rest of the day. I apply what I read to the rest of my day, and try to use it to motivate and inspire those around me. Often, I will post a verse or quote on Twitter or Facebook on what I read in the morning. I allow these teachings from my Bible to feed my mind and my heart and influence my actions from the morning to the entire day. This is not only my routine during the work week either. Even on the weekends, I seem to not be able to really lay in bed for very long. I am simply not the type to sleep in. My body will essentially force me to get up and do something with my day.

For this reason, I feel as if each day is already set out and planned out before I even make it to the office. I also feel awake first thing in the morning, as opposed to others who seem to be still groggy during the first hour or so of work. This extra hour of awake and aware work, paired with the fact that I have been up already planning my method of attack on the day's tasks, will provide me with a leg up on the competition who is still awake and unprepared when they arrive to the office. This boosts my effectiveness in the mornings as well as my efficiency overall. Think about having an extra hour a day for you to get work-related projects finished. Anyone who is actively working on a large task knows that an hour is not that much time. But every day of the average work week? That is five extra hours a week, just three hours short of a normal day. What if we do this all month long? Well, that would be an extra twenty hours for the week! Half of the average 40 hour work week!

What could you accomplish in an extra twenty hours? What if instead of waking up an hour early for a month, you do it for a year? Well, that would average out to two hundred and forty extra hours a year, if we do not count holidays. This would work out to an extra six weeks in our year of strictly planning and preparation time! You could get a run or quick work out in before work, like some of the leaders mentioned previously do. You could check your emails and texts and get a mental jump-start on the day like I tend to do myself, or you could have a good breakfast and get yourself to relax before you show up and start the day. The possibilities are endless.

It boils down to one hour. Everyone has it. You will make the time in your life for the things that you really want to do. One hour. 60 minutes. 3,600 seconds. This one hour every day that will allow you six weeks of extra time that you were previously wasting. The 1800's era economist, Richard Whately had a quote about this concept. Whately once stated:

"Lose an hour in the morning, and you will spend all day looking for it."

Think about any time in your life that you were unable to hit a deadline. Maybe you had a project that needed to be finished that you came up short on. Maybe as a college student, you were unable to submit a project or a test in time and failed it. What if you had woken up early? Would that hour have helped you at the time? Maybe you needed more than an hour, could you have finished it then?

Instead of hitting snooze and going back to bed, get up! Hitting snooze on your alarm is like hitting snooze on your dreams. It is like the shopper who walks into a retail store and says, "I'll be back" to the employee of the store. You won't be! Commit to it. Declare it yourself that you will get up earlier and use the time that God has provided you with in order to make your dream a reality.

One of the worst things that could ever happen when you pass away and your soul leaves this world, would be having God show you the person that you could have been, if only you had tried. If you had devoted more time to your craft, more effort, if you had studied more, or worked at it with a little more hunger. To me, that is a scary thought to have. You do not want to ever wonder or be curious about what you COULD have done. Go do it! Find out just what it is that you are capable as a person and as a leader. The only way to find this out, is do give it your best. You do not have time for slacking off. Sleep is for the weak. You can either sleep and let your dreams stay dreams, or you can wake up, put your shoes on, and chase them.

Aristotle, like Richard Whately, made comments on the importance of waking up early. He said that:

"It is well to be up before daybreak, for such habits contribute to health, wealth and wisdom."

Aristotle believed this extra time that you will utilize by getting up earlier than most will provide you with the opportunities to work and earn money, lead a healthier lifestyle, and learn much more about yourself and the world around you. There is a fine line between want and need and, when it comes to sleep, chances are, you want more of it than you actually need. Your own dreams and passions (and perhaps a little help from your coffee!) should be enough to get you out of bed, keep you up at night, get you excited to come to work, and excited for the next day as you leave the office!

It is true, however, that being an early riser or one who sleeps in can run in your genes. If your parents were the type to sleep in, there will be a good chance that you follow suit. Just as my father is an early riser, so am I. However, being more predisposed to a specific pattern or behavior does not mean that you cannot change that habit. I implore you to set your alarm a little bit early. Lay your outfit out the night before, make sure you have things set up for when you wake up in the morning. Set little reminders for yourself to get to bed just a little bit earlier than you normally do. I think that it would do wonders for those reading who are not "morning people" by nature, to get up and out of bed an hour earlier for just thirty days. See if it helps, and see the change in the way you begin to feel when you get into the office. Do you feel more clear-headed? Not as groggy or cloudy or scatterbrained as you usually feel? If so, and if you feel as if you are getting much more done than normal, then do not stop at thirty days! Make this your normal morning routine.

Another benefit that I receive from getting up and getting ready for my day so early is the fact that I am rarely behind schedule. When you wake up an hour earlier than you need to, it makes getting to work or getting your kids to school much easier. There is no stress of having to rush to appointments or to the office because you are already good to go! By having a set schedule and getting up early regularly, you will not be as slow and sluggish in the morning. You will not lag behind and as such, will move at a pace that will allow you to be on time and be ready to go when you arrive to the office. This will help you manage your overall stress level, as well as help to set the pace for how your day will be.

It is also said by some that those who sleep for ten or more hours in one night seem to take much longer to fall asleep. They will often toss and turn, and wake up multiple times throughout the night. Often, people who sleep for too long will state that they feel fatigued throughout the day. People whose sleeping schedule tends to vary greatly also report to have this issue. Staying mindful and being on top of your sleeping patterns can have a drastic effect on both your health as well as your performance and levels of productivity. I am not saying that you have to be as firm and militant about your schedule as

Benjamin Franklin was, as life is unpredictable and things come up. But you do need to be wary of the amount of rest that you are actually getting. It is wise to be the type of person who is early to bed and early to rise. It is good to get the amount of sleep that your own body needs, but it can be very detrimental to you if you are simply lying in bed for ten hours or more at a time. Get up, get active, get motivated, and get productive.

To put it mildly, those who sleep longer than eight hours at a given time statistically have higher reported levels of stress. A strong argument could be made that this is a direct result of a person not having enough time to complete daily tasks and being stressed out from running behind so often. Higher levels of stress can lead to heart disease, weight gain, stroke, high blood pressure, and diabetes. It is not only productive in the workplace for you to wake up early, but it is good for your health! Instead of running by McDonald's on the way to work, you have the time and opportunity to eat something more nutritional before you head out. Instead of lying in bed, you can head to the gym before it is time for work. All of these are choices that you make each and every day, and they can have a profound effect on your mood, attitude towards the day, your physical and mental health, and your levels of productivity once you have reached your place of business.

Do not catch yourself sleeping when your competitor is training. Much like a boxing match, the fighter who is better prepared and in better shape, the one who spent countless hours getting ready for this match, THAT is the guy who usually wins. The one who showed up late and out of shape and was unprepared to fight will surely lose. Don't be that guy! Prepare yourself now, so you do not have to rush later. Use your time wisely. Understand that leadership is a state of being, not a job. You do not stop being a leader when you clock out and go home. You are a leader. When you wake up and your head comes off of your pillow and your feet touch the ground, you are going to have to get in the work mode, and lead. If you are not viewing your job as a leader in this way, you need to reevaluate your definition of passion. If this is your passion, it should be enough to get you up and to keep you up. If this is what you dream about then wake up and go accomplish it.

I will not allow myself to be caught sleeping on the job. When there is work that needs to be done, there is no time for sleep, and there is always work to be done. A lot of people wish for the opportunity to have more time, and this is the opportunity now. Get up early and expedite the planning and preparing process, that way you will have more time during the actual work process. We discussed efficiency and the importance of it previously in this book, and this is a surefire way to boost your own personal level of efficiency in nearly every aspect of your life. There is no time to sleep half of the day away when there is a whole world out there for you to experience. We have no time for sitting down and being still when there are so many possibilities and obstacles and tasks for you to accomplish and overcome.

It is a popular saying that if you do not take the time out of your life to start building your own dreams, then someone will hire you to build theirs. By saving and cherishing every minute that the Lord has blessed you with, and using this precious time to work on the things that you need to work on, you will have a much better opportunity to reach the level of success that you desire as a leader and as a person.

By getting yourself into the correct, positive frame of mind early when you get up and begin to get ready for your day, you will reach newfound heights of efficiency, effectiveness, and most importantly, happiness. Your work will feel easier, your stress levels will be at an all–time low, and it will not go unnoticed by your team. It is wise to become an early riser if you are not one already. Get up, read your Bible, check your emails, get in a quick workout, eat a healthy breakfast, do whatever it is that gets you into the mindset that you need to be in as a leader. Be the early bird.

And go get that worm.

"My eyes are awake before the watches of the night, that I may meditate on your promise" – Psalms 119:148

CHAPTER 10

I Can. I Will. End of Story.

"I will persist until I succeed. I was not delivered unto this world in defeat, nor does failure flow through my veins." – Og Mandino

It has been said that those who say they can and those who say they cannot are both correct. Some of us do not realize how much power words can actually have on us. Do not let them fool you. Just because words are not a physical or tangible substance does not mean that they do not have the potential to seriously impact our perception of our surroundings, our team, and our lives. The old phrase that we were taught as kids about sticks and stones breaking our bones but words will not hurt us is simply false. Sticks and stones can break down our bodies. Words will break down our hearts, minds, and spirits. You will become whatever it is that you think about all day. If failure and self-doubt is what you focus on, it will be your destiny. But God himself has bigger plans for you, as a leader and as a person.

One secret to leading a successful and fulfilling life is to choose the correct words to use. By using the correct words that have a positive connotation, it will allow us to view the world through a more positive and proper perspective. This will, in turn, allow us to bring out the absolute best in ourselves as leaders. By keeping a positive attitude and keeping a cool head, we will become a version of us that is unimaginable. We need positive words and vibes to persevere through the many rough patches that we all (especially as leaders) will be faced with. These words of encouragement from ourselves will help to be our guides through the terrain that we will face on the journey from minor success, to great significance. One word that I hear people use often is "can't."

I can't. It is impossible. There is no way. These are phrases used by people who do not have belief in themselves. Stop using these words! "I can't" is said by others to admit their lack of skill or to show that they have a lack of faith in their own power. Distance yourself from that phrase. If you believe it, you can achieve it. You can do it. You must first try.

"It is impossible" is a phrase that simply means that something has never been done before. Flying used to be believed to be impossible, until Wilbur and Orville Wright built and successful flew the very first airplane back in 1903. Remember when we discussed Steve Jobs? Before him and his contributions to Apple, the idea that every household could have a reliable computer for personal use was extremely far-fetched, to say the least. Before Henry Ford, the idea of producing even more than just a handful of automobiles a day was "impossible." Back in the 1950s, the idea that we as a nation would be putting people on the moon instead of just satellites into space was unheard of. Impossible is not fact. In many causes, impossible is the biggest lie. Everything is viewed as "impossible" until someone does it. Everything is viewed as "crazy" until it ends up working. It is possible. You must first put in the effort.

"There is no way" only means that you have not yet found a way. A way to your dreams, to your vision, to follow your passion, or maybe a way to simply complete your tasks. There is always a way. You must find it.

Eliminate these three phrases! Take your vocabulary book, open it up, and dump "I can't" and "it is impossible" and "there is no way" into the trash can. Saying these things to yourself or about yourself to those around you in any situation is singlehandedly the most common and most harmful form of self-affliction on Earth. You might as well stop trying at whatever you are doing if you truly believe in one of these three phrases. Life is about breaking through the walls of "I can't" or "it is impossible" or "there is no way." You CAN. It IS possible. There IS a way.

Simply thinking that you cannot do something will instantly weaken you. It is impossible to get through anything if you truly do not believe that you can accomplish the task which is at hand. Simply telling yourself that you are unable to overcome that which life has thrown at you will keep you in a rut, too afraid to try and break out of a boring and average lifestyle.

To break out of this, you must take risks. Without risk, there will be no reward. Those who build themselves up and tell themselves that they are ABLE to overcome the many obstacles life will put in their way will surely do so. You must understand that the only person who has the power to stop you from being successful, is yourself. You will never truly know what you are capable of accomplishing in your life until you try your absolute best. Wayne Gretzsky once said:

"You will miss one hundred of the shots that you don't take."

The saying proves true in more aspects than just hockey. If you do not try, you will spend the rest of your life wondering what could have been. I don't know about you, but I do not want to reach the end of my lifetime wishing that I would have tried to push myself a little bit further. I do not want to spend my days wondering what could have or should have been if I had the chance to do it all over again.

Self-doubt and being unsure and indecisive can potentially stop you from changing not only yourself or your organization, but the world. Think about it: If Nikola Tesla grew tired and gave up on his work, if Walt Disney was discouraged and never tried to make it in the animation and art world, if Henry Ford gave up when his first business was unsuccessful, and if Michael Jordan stopped playing basketball back in high school when he did not make the team where would the world be? Can you imagine how different the world would look without proper electric power? What about a world without Disney and without the addition of sound in cartoons, or the advancements in the animation world? The auto assembly line made it possible for everyone to own an automobile, what if it never existed? I, for one, am a huge sports fan and cannot fathom what it would have been like to miss out on watching Michael Jordan play. Charles R. Swindoll has a quote that I have mentioned countless times in my leadership meetings at iPD. He said:

"The longer I live, the more I realize the effect that attitude has on my life."

It is only very recently, after all of this time, that I have begun to understand what exactly he means by that statement. Your attitude towards your team, towards yourself, your situations, and your own challenges–these things can make a huge difference in the way your organization turns out. They make a difference in the way that your life outside of the office or workplace turns out as well. If you stop and think about this fact, and you truly can internalize that as a leader, I believe that you may start to view things much differently than you may view them now.

These people, these leaders in their respected fields, made decisions in their lives. They could give up and spend the rest of their days wondering, or they could try, even in the face of what was almost certain defeat. The rest of their stories are marked down in history and written amongst the stars. God had plans for these individuals that were greater than even they could fathom. Imagine going back and telling the Michael Jordan that just got cut from his high school team, that he would go on to be arguably the greatest player who ever stepped onto an NBA court. Or explaining to a discouraged and dejected Walt Disney that no one would know the newspaper company that fired him for "lacking imagination," but that his imagination would change the lives and childhood of every person in America. What makes you and I different from them?

One major thing: choices. The choice to ignore the sound of self-doubt. The choice to take that voice inside your head and shut it up so you can think. People will say what they will in effort to tempt you to quit or tear down your idea, but all that matters is what you believe. If you believe that you can achieve it, then God will make it so. If it is something that you are unsure of or not fully committed to, then it will not prosper. Release your doubts. Release your insecurities. Release every reason why you have determined that what you are attempting to accomplish will fail.

There is no time in life for self-doubt. There is no time in life for wondering what could be and not doing anything about it. It is time to step up to the plate. To get off of the bench and onto the field like we discussed back in the very first chapter. If you see the world not for what it is, but for what it could be, do not sit around and wait for the person who will come and change it. Be the person! The world needs more people like you who will step up and do it while others around you watch and think about it. Winners never quit, and quitters have never won. Understand that nothing changes, if nothing changes. If you are not actively changing and actually trying to accomplish something, then it will surely not be accomplished. You cannot be afraid of failure. You cannot be petrified with fear and self-doubt. Understand that while you should listen to your instincts, you should not listen to your fears.

Even the individuals who appear to be the most confident can be attacked with thoughts of self-doubt. Can I really do this? Will this really work? Is this something that I am capable of?

These questions are common for anyone who is starting something new or venturing into the unknown. Fear and self-doubt go hand-in-hand. Fear of coming up short and fear of not being enough is the direct cause of self-doubt.

I believe that there are times in life where you have to kick your fear in the teeth. You have to beat it down. Block it out. Ignore it. You see, we have the power within ourselves to destroy our fears. Sometimes the greatest opportunities in your life are shrouded by fear and mystery. Sometimes the greatest and most fulfilling rewards in life come just after the point of fear. When you first ride a rollercoaster, chances are, you are terrified. You tighten the buckles or the straps down as tightly as possible. You contemplate yelling out for the workers of the ride to shut it down and let you off. You grip the lap bar tightly, and then you go for a ride and find out how much fun it can be. You would have never had the experience if you listened to your fears and your doubts.

Another example would be when you jump into the pool and learn to swim for the first time like I discussed at the start of this book with my own children. To put it mildly, you are terrified. Walking over to the edge. Staring back into the water, wondering how it is going to go for you. It does not matter who is in the pool, or whether you have any floats to cling to, you are scared. My kids were unsure as to whether I would be able to help. They were unsure if they had it within themselves to accomplish this feat. But, like the kid learning to swim, you must first try. This is true for the office, for any type of sport, any trade that you may be interested in learning, you cannot let your self doubt dictate what you do in your lifetime. By allowing fears to rule your world, you may never find what it is that you are truly passionate about. You may never gain the opportunity to discover some of the gifts that God himself has instilled in you. To miss out on these experiences is to waste your life. The late Leo Buscaglia, whom I have referenced previously, spoke about this topic once.

Leo Buscaglia said:

"The day you are born, you are given the world as your birthday present. It frightens me that so few people even bother to open up the ribbon."

By this, he was talking about all of the different people that he met on his journey as a speaker. He saw people who would confess to him their pain and their feelings of self-loathing and self-doubt. He saw great things in these people, and hated the idea that they could not see them themselves and utilize them to their advantage. I tend to agree. The purpose of this book is to coach and to help other leaders understand that in order to speed up their journey to being stronger leaders, you must first look within yourself before working on your team.

Look inside yourself. Understand what it is that you do best. Understand the qualities that God has blessed you with and know that you cannot be afraid or lazy or insecure. You can do this. You can bring your team to newfound heights. You can bring yourself to places that you had never thought were possible. As a leader, you will be unable to convince anyone on your team of anything if you do not believe it yourself. If you do not believe that you as a team will be able to achieve the goals that you wanted to achieve, no one on your team will think it is possible either. People can pick up on when someone is not completely involved. You can fool some, but you will never fool all. Therefore, you as a leader take an extreme amount of care, and consider those around you before you throw words like "can't" or "impossible" or "unable" around. To lead, you must be positive. Have a positive outlook rather than a negative one. Be an optimist and not a pessimist.

Understand that negative ways of thinking and pessimistic mindsets are contagious. But also understand that positive ways of thinking and optimistic mindsets are, too. Use this to your advantage. Be the leader that you may have wished that you had early on in your career. Instill in your team that they, as a unit, are unstoppable when it comes to doing what they do best. We will have to make sure our team believes it as well, and the only way for them to believe it, is for you to believe it when you tell them.

I wanted to take this time to reflect on the themes that are in each chapter of this book, as well as why I decided to format it in such a manner. In chapter one, we discussed the importance of getting off of the bench. Of getting up and actually trying, as it is the first step in success. You must start the race before you can win the race.

In chapter two, we went over the importance of having your team together on the same page, striving towards the same goals. By having everyone in the organization working to accomplish the same basic task, you have a better shot at success. Great minds think alike, and two or more heads are much better than one.

In chapter three, we went over how we, as leaders, will be solely in charge of finding out how the individuals in your team fit with one another. You must take care to put the pieces together in a way that will be helpful and not detrimental to your company. Understand how each department works, and how they can benefit the organization as a whole. Take note of the importance of every member of the group.

In chapter four, we discussed the concepts of changing and transforming, both as a leader as well as an entire organization. We, as leaders of change, must embrace change and view it as necessary in order to flourish, if we have any hopes of our team welcoming change with a positive attitude. Changes will come, and we have to be ready for them.

In chapter five, we went over the importance of being the best version of you that you can possibly be. We discussed, in detail, the need for you as a leader to utilize both your strengths as well as your own individuality. By being original and using your own natural abilities in order to assist your team, you will build them up and properly lead them down the right path.

We followed up chapter five's talks about strength, with chapter six. Chapter six discussed weaknesses and failures and how you should take them as a leader. Let your failures and your weaknesses not discourage you but encourage and motivate you to get stronger. Leaders will fail and fail again before they succeed, and you must prepare yourself mentally for failure and weaknesses to come.

In chapter seven, we went into the idea that in order to be a successful leader, we must also learn to properly teach our team. For some leaders, this may come naturally, while others will struggle at first with understanding how to teach their team. Remember that different types of people will learn in a variety of different ways, and it will be up to you to figure out what works for each person in your respected team.

In chapter eight, we talked about ways for us as leaders to lead effectively as well as efficiently. The most important job as a leader is simple: to lead. We must find ways to effectively reach and captivate our team when going over various subjects in the workplace. Once we have perfected our effectiveness, we must strive to be a more efficient leader. Find ways to get more work done in less time. Teach these methods to your team, who will in turn implement them in their own daily lives. Be open to their ideas for better efficiency. As a more effective and efficient leader, you will path the way for a more effective and efficient organization as a whole.

Being a great leader takes a lot out of you, some of which I have spoke about here in this book. But being a leader will also put a lot back in. You will gain knowledge, understanding and have empathy of those who you work in close quarters with. You will see your team at their absolute best, and their absolute worst. We must take care to know when to do what, and how to assist them at all times. We are leaders. We uplift, we train, we strengthen, and then we repeat the process. For the leaders who are still with me, I write this to explain that being a leader is not easy.

There are many qualities and traits involved, but above all else, it takes a solid work ethic, a large vision, an extreme level of determination. It takes an unwavering faith, and a unique, strong love of people. With these traits, you will learn to lead rather than becoming lunch. With these traits, you will learn how to earn the influence of those around you, and gain the power that comes as a result of it.

One of my inspirations for this book was a book by John Maxwell titled "How To Develop A Leader Within You" which I believe had a profound effect on me, both as a person as well as a leader in my own areas of expertise. I implore those who read this and feel like they took something from it to read it. As I have described throughout this novel, being a leader will come with rewards as well as setbacks, Ultimately, you must always be moving, always striving to reach the next goal, the next destination, the next opportunity. Your craft will never be perfected and you will always be striving for improvement. As long as you keep this concept in mind, and strive to better the organization for not just you, but for the others who rely on you to be led, you will come out alright.

Find your passion as a leader, and utilize the strengths that the Lord has given to you in order to make your dreams and vi-sions a reality. Do not be discouraged by the idea of failure, or the various thoughts of self-doubt that may plague your mind. You must not waste your time and energy discussing large plans with small-minded people. It will only create a toxic environment and an unsure mind to associate with those who do not believe in your vision. You cannot let others put you down and discourage you from even attempting to accomplish what you want to get done.

In short, to succeed you must get off of the bench. You must understand the importance of having a culture of purpose. You, as a leader of change, must understand how to put the pieces together when dealing with your team members directly. You must be prepared and be okay with changing and transforming, not only with yourself but with your organization as a whole. You, as a leader, must be yourself, but be your best self. You will need to understand how you can be fueled by failure, rather than get discouraged and defeated by it. You will have to understand and find ways to be able to properly teach those around you, and realize that it will need to most likely be with a different approach for each person who is involved with the organization, as people learn in many different ways. You will ultimately need to learn how to lead effectively and efficiently amongst the rest of your group, making sure everyone is on the same page and ready to attack whatever task or obstacle that they find in front of them, as a team. You will have to take into account how you speak to your team, how to convey what it is that you are trying to teach them in a way that everyone knows what is going on and what they will be facing. You will also need to know what is in your hands. What you have in front of you, the tools, which will sometimes be individuals and other times be a matter of situation. You will also need to understand that which you will be able to change, and how to counteract outside forces in which you may not be able to necessarily control. Understand that with a solid mindset and a strong team who strives for success just as hard and diligently as you do, that you will be able to be successful. It all starts with one person, and that is you.

These are the ways that I myself have become a successful leader in my own industry. These are the ways that I run my own business day-in and day-out. I truly hope that you will be able to make some sense of it, take these tools provided in these few chapters, and implement them within your own life.

"Forget the former things; do not dwell on the past. See, I am doing a new thing! Now it springs up, do you not perceive it? I am making a way in the wilderness and streams in the wasteland." – Isaiah 43:18–19